Easy, SWEET, & SUGARFREE

"An easy and delicious way to have some of those sweets with absolutely no added sugar, honey or artificial sweeteners."
—Portland Oregonian

"Those who love their sweets and still want to remain well . . . will love this book."
—A. Hoffer, M.D., Ph. D., author of Orthomolecular Nutrition and Nutrients to Age without Senility

"Tasty and elegant. Easy, Sweet & Sugarfree will satisfy both the conscience and the sweet tooth."   —The Newton (Ct.) Bee

"Barkie has worked hard and effectively to add cheer to the lives of those who love desserts but must or want to avoid both sugar and artificial sweeteners."   —Library Journal

"Barkie . . . succeeds in creating desserts that are both appealing and nutritious."   —Beatrice Trum Hunter, author of The Sugar Trap & How to Avoid It

Easy, SWEET, & SUGARFREE

KAREN E. BARKIE

Originally published in hardcover as
Fancy, Sweet & Sugarfree

ST. MARTIN'S PRESS/NEW YORK

Originally published in hardcover as *Fancy, Sweet & Sugarfree*

EASY, SWEET & SUGARFREE

Copyright © 1985 by Karen E. Barkie

Library of Congress Catalog Card Number: 84-24976

ISBN: 0-312-90282-4   Can. ISBN: 0-312-90283-2

Printed in the United States of America

First St. Martin's Press mass market edition/June 1987

10   9   8   7   6   5   4   3   2   1

To my husband, Bob,
for his support,
encouragement,
and love

CONTENTS

INTRODUCTION

Americans love rich and sweet desserts. What would Thanksgiving be without pumpkin pie, Christmas without candy, and birthdays without cake and ice cream? We always have room for "a little more," "just one bite," and often for a far more generous helping than originally intended. There's no getting away from it—we're happily hooked on desserts.

But they don't have to be our downfall—the times we cheat on our diets, eat sugary foods we're supposed to avoid, indulge in something we shouldn't. Desserts don't have to be the least nutritious part of our meals; what we love the most doesn't have to be the worst for us. Fruit-sweetening has changed all this.

Fruit is the ideal sweetener. In contrast to sugar, which is highly refined (99.9 percent pure sucrose), fruit is natural. It is an excellent source of fiber, vitamins, and minerals, and highly recommended as a source of vitamin A, vitamin C, and B vitamins. Sugar is so refined that all the vitamins and minerals are removed, making it simply a source of empty calories. And if you're watching calories, you'll be happy to know that one cup of chopped fresh fruit has only about 11 percent of the calories in an equal measure of sugar.

Fruit is an even more nutritious sweetener than honey. Although honey is a natural product, containing some vitamins and minerals, these nutrients exist in small amounts. It would take 5 cups of honey to meet your daily recommended requirement of potassium, 16½ cups for phosphorus, and 12½ cups for calcium. While honey contains no vitamin A, cantaloupes, apricots, papayas, and mangoes are good sources. Lemons, oranges, guavas, papayas, and strawberries supply at least 50 times the vitamin C in an equivalent weight of honey. Many fruits, including bananas, limes, lemons, and persimmons, are richer in iron than honey is. Furthermore, the B vitamins, fiber, and various minerals found in limited quantities in honey are abundant in many fruits.

Besides being more nutritious than honey, fruit is far lower in calories. Compared pound per pound, few fruits contain more than 20 percent of the calories in an equal weight of honey. One cup of honey at 992 calories has even more calories than one cup of sugar at 751. On the average, one cup of chopped fresh fruit has a modest 82 calories.

As well as being more nutritious and lower in calories than sugar or honey, fruit has other advantages. It is a remarkably versatile sweetener, available in a wide variety of forms. Fruit-sweetening may be introduced into desserts through fruit juices, frozen fruit juice concentrates, chopped fresh fruit, canned fruit, fruit purées, chopped dried fruit, and sliced frozen fruit—all unsweetened. It has the added advantage of contributing not only sweetness, but also a wide array of delicious flavors to desserts. No other sweetener imparts the refreshing tang of pineapple, or earthy spice of applesauce, or light sweetness of orange juice. Furthermore, fruit is naturally concentrated, not unnaturally sweet like sugar, so it blends readily with other ingredients. It adds sweetness and flavor without overpowering and masking extracts, spices, and other flavorings.

Over five years of work in the field of fruit-sweetening has only heightened my enthusiasm and conviction that fruit is the ideal sweetener. In 1982 my first fruit-sweetened dessert cookbook, *Sweet and Sugarfree,* was released. The response was overwhelming, with over 100,000 books sold in the first 18 months, and sales are still climbing. Americans are ready to take desserts seriously, to demand good nutrition as well as taste, and to use the sweetener that supplies both: fruit.

Easy, Sweet, & Sugarfree is a collection of more original recipes. Desserts are light and more flavorful, with a selection of luscious toppings, glazes, and icings. I've used frozen fruit-juice concentrates to enhance natural sweetness rather than fruit juices that give a lighter sweetness. I've tried to produce a collection of the highest quality desserts to serve for all occasions. Guidelines for adapting recipes to special dietary requirements are included so that those on restricted diets may also enjoy fruit-sweetened desserts. Information for those with sugar sensitivities, allergies, or hyperactivity, and for the growing population on low-calorie or cholesterol-restricted diets, will allow everyone to enjoy and use these recipes.

Fruit-sweetening opens up a whole new field in dessert sweetening. It transforms sugary desserts into sugarfree ones, high-calorie desserts into low-calorie treats, unhealthful desserts into nutritious complements to our meals. And just as important as all the good nutrition fruit brings to desserts, fruit-sweetened desserts taste delicious as well. Try them and see!

Author's Note

All the ingredients used in this book are available in unsweetened form. Choose ingredients carefully, as sugar may be added by the manufacturer to many otherwise sugarfree products. READ LA-BELS.

Cakes

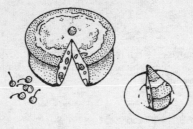

PINEAPPLE POUND CAKE

A flavorful, moist loaf cake topped with rich Pineapple-Cocoa Icing.

CAKE:
½ cup butter, softened (or shortening)
3 large eggs
½ cup unsweetened frozen pineapple juice concentrate, thawed
½ cup water

2½ cups unbleached white flour
1 teaspoon baking soda
1 teaspoon baking powder

ICING:
Pineapple-Cocoa Icing (see page 111)

In a large mixing bowl beat together butter (or shortening), eggs, pineapple juice concentrate, and water until thoroughly blended. Add flour, baking soda, and baking powder; beat just until blended.

Spoon mixture evenly into a 9" by 5" oiled and floured loaf pan. Bake in a preheated oven at 350 degrees for 45 minutes or until a knife inserted comes out clean. Cool on a wire rack.

Prepare icing as directed. Slide a plate under the wire rack to catch icing, and generously spoon icing over cake. Completely cover top and allow icing to drip down sides. Refrigerate to set icing. When icing has set wrap in foil or plastic wrap and store refrigerated until serving.

Serves 6 to 8.

ORANGE CREAM ROLL

This light orange cake roll is generously filled with whipped cream and blueberries. If blueberries are not available, simply substitute your favorite fruit.

CAKE:
1 cup unbleached white flour
¼ teaspoon baking soda
4 large eggs, separated (room temperature)
⅓ cup unsweetened frozen orange juice concentrate, thawed
1 teaspoon vanilla extract

FILLING:
Creamy Topping (see page 104)
1 cup fresh blueberries (or other fresh fruit)

TOPPING:
¼ teaspoon grated orange rind

To prepare cake, line a 10″ by 14″ jelly roll pan with wax paper and butter. Set aside.

In a small bowl mix together flour and baking soda; set aside. Beat egg yolks at high speed in a small bowl for 5 minutes until thick and lemon colored. Beat in orange juice concentrate and vanilla extract. Fold in flour mixture. Beat egg whites until thick and peaks hold their shape. Add juice mixture and fold together gently but thoroughly. Spoon batter into buttered jelly roll pan and spread evenly in pan. Bake in a preheated oven at 325 degrees for 12 minutes. Remove from the oven. With a sharp knife loosen edges and cut off any crisp edges. Turn cake out onto a clean linen towel, and gently peel off wax paper.

Starting at the shorter end, loosely roll up cake and towel. Cool on a wire rack for 10 minutes. Carefully unroll, remove towel, reroll, and allow to cool on a wire rack.

For filling, prepare Creamy Topping as directed and fold in blueberries. Gently unroll cake. Reserving ¼ cup filling, spread the remaining filling evenly over cake. Slowly reroll cake. Wrap securely in foil and store refrigerated.

To serve, place roll on serving platter. Top with reserved filling and sprinkle with grated orange rind. May be garnished with colorful fresh fruit if desired. Slice into 1"-wide slices.

Serves 8 to 10.

FLORIDA SUNSHINE CAKE

A delicious combination—sweet orange cake filled with fruit and smothered with a cold pineapple cream frosting.

CAKE:
½ cup butter, softened (or shortening)
3 large eggs
½ cup unsweetened frozen orange juice concentrate, thawed
½ cup water
1 teaspoon orange extract
2½ cups unbleached white flour
1 teaspoon baking soda
1 teaspoon baking powder

FROSTING:
2 tablespoons unflavored gelatin (2 packets)

½ cup cold water
3½ cups unsweetened pineapple juice
Creamy Topping (see page 104)

FILLING:
1 banana (about 1 cup, sliced)
1 medium-sized (16 oz.) can orange segments in unsweetened juice (or 1⅓ cups fresh orange segments)
1 small (8 oz.) can tangerine segments in unsweetened juice
1 fresh kiwi fruit (optional)

To prepare cake, beat together butter (or shortening), eggs, orange juice concentrate, water, and orange extract. Add flour, baking soda, and baking powder; beat well. Divide batter equally into 2 oiled and floured 9" by 1½" round baking pans. Smooth batter in pans. Bake in a preheated oven at 350 degrees for 15 minutes or until a knife inserted comes out clean. Allow cakes to cool in pans 5 minutes before turning out onto wire racks to cool completely. Wrap individually in plastic wrap or foil and store refrigerated.

To prepare frosting, sprinkle gelatin over water in a small bowl. Allow to soften for 5 minutes. Meanwhile, bring pineapple juice to a boil. (If using fresh or frozen pineapple juice it must be boiled 3 minutes to destroy an enzyme that interferes with proper gelation.) Then, stir in softened gelatin, cool, and refrigerate until mixture reaches a consistency slightly thicker than unbeaten egg whites. Prepare Creamy Topping as directed and fold into gelatin mixture.

To assemble cake, place 1 chilled cake layer in the center of a 9" springform pan, leaving ¼" of space between cake and pan edge all around. Spoon gelatin frosting around cake edges, pushing frosting into crevice with a knife. Spread a thin layer of frosting over cake. Top evenly with sliced banana and drained orange segments, stopping about ¼" from cake edges. Spread a thin layer of frosting over filling. Top with second cake layer, centering it in the pan and gently pressing down. Frost edges as directed previously and top with remaining frosting. Garnish top with well-drained tangerine segments and sliced kiwi fruit, or your choice of colorful fruit. Refrigerate until set.

To serve, loosen edges from pan with a sharp knife. Remove sides. Slide cake, metal bottom attached, onto serving dish. Serving dish may be garnished with additional fruit.

Serves 8 to 12.

CHERRY ORANGE CHIFFON CAKE

A light sponge cake laced with diced cherries.

CAKE:
7 large eggs, separated (room temperature)
1 6-oz. can unsweetened frozen orange juice concentrate, thawed
1 teaspoon vanilla extract
½ teaspoon orange extract
1 tablespoon lemon juice

1½ cups unbleached white flour
¼ teaspoon salt
1¼ teaspoons cream of tartar
¼ cup finely diced sweet cherries (approximately 6 cherries)

FROSTING:
Creamy Frosting (see page 105)

Beat egg yolks at high speed for 5 minutes until thick and lemon colored; set aside. In a small bowl combine orange juice concentrate, vanilla extract, orange extract, and lemon juice; set aside. In another small bowl toss together flour and salt. Gradually add orange mixture and flour mixture alternately to beaten egg yolks. Mix well.

With clean beaters, beat egg whites until foamy. Add cream of tartar, and beat until quite firm. (Do not underbeat.) Gently fold orange mixture into egg whites, mixing just until streaks of egg white disappear. Gradually sprinkle in diced cherries. Spoon mixture into an ungreased 10" tube pan. Cut into batter with a knife to release any air bubbles. Smooth top. Bake in a preheated oven at 325 degrees for 55 to 60 minutes or until well browned and very firm to the touch. Invert pan over a bottle and allow to cool. When completely cooled, loosen edges with a sharp knife. Remove pan. Invert on serving dish.

Prepare Creamy Frosting as directed and frost cake. May be garnished with sliced fresh cherries.

Serves 8 to 10.

• *Note:* Do not substitute pineapple juice, as it does not work in the above recipe.

ORANGE RING WITH CHOCOLATE ICING

A light orange tube cake covered with a chocolaty icing and garnished with orange segments.

CAKE:
3 large eggs
½ cup butter, softened (or shortening)
⅓ cup unsweetened frozen orange juice concentrate, thawed
¾ cup water
2½ cups unbleached white flour
1 teaspoon baking soda

1 teaspoon baking powder

ICING:
Chocolate Icing (see page 110)

GARNISH:
1 small (8 oz.) can orange segments in unsweetened juice

Beat together eggs, butter (or shortening), orange juice concentrate, and water until thoroughly blended. Add flour, baking soda, and baking powder; beat well. Spoon mixture evenly into an oiled and floured 9" tube pan. Bake in a preheated oven at 350 degrees for 30 minutes or until a knife inserted comes out clean. Cool cake 10 minutes in the pan before loosening edges and turning out on a wire rack.

Prepare icing as directed. Place rack holding cake over a plate and generously spoon warm icing over the cake, allowing icing to attractively drip down sides.

Drain juice from can of orange segments and arrange segments in a ring along cake top. Refrigerate to set.

Serves 6 to 8.

FRESH STRAWBERRY FLAN

A large flat cake covered with a thin layer of cream cheese and topped with whole fresh red strawberries.

CAKE:
4 large eggs, separated (room temperature)
1/3 cup unsweetened frozen pineapple juice concentrate, thawed
2 teaspoons vanilla extract
1 cup unbleached white flour
1/4 teaspoon baking soda

FILLING:
1 8-oz. package cream cheese, softened
2 tablespoons milk
1 teaspoon vanilla extract

TOPPING:
2 pints fresh strawberries

GARNISH:
Cream Cheese Rosettes (see page 108)

To prepare cake, beat egg yolks at high speed for at least 5 minutes; mixture will be thick and lemon colored. Add pineapple juice concentrate and vanilla extract. Beat thoroughly. Gradually fold in flour mixed with baking soda; set aside.

Whip egg whites at high speed until quite thick and stiff. Add liquid mixture and fold together until evenly blended. Spoon mixture into an 11" pie or cake pan that has been lined with buttered aluminum foil. Spread batter evenly in pan. Bake in a preheated oven at 325 degrees for 12 minutes. Cake will be firm to the touch. Remove cake from the oven and allow to cool in the pan 10 minutes. Cover cake with a large wire rack and flip over. Remove pan. Carefully pry off foil, and allow cake to cool. Cover cooled cake with a large serving dish, invert, and gently remove wire rack.

Beat together filling ingredients until smooth. Spread evenly over cake, stopping 1/4" from the edge. Slice stems off strawberries. Place top side down over the top of the cake, completely covering cream cheese topping. Decorate outside edges with Cream Cheese Rosettes as directed.

To serve, cut into pie-shaped wedges.

Serves 8 to 10.

SUNNY CITRUS SQUARES

A thin layer of cake generously topped with pineapple gel and colorful orange segments—how sweet it is!

CAKE:
1/4 cup butter, softened (or shortening)
2 large eggs
1/4 teaspoon orange extract
1 teaspoon lemon juice
1/2 cup unsweetened frozen pineapple-orange juice concentrate, thawed
1 cup unbleached white flour

1/4 teaspoon baking soda
1/4 teaspoon baking powder

TOPPING:
2 cups unsweetened pineapple juice
1/4 cup cornstarch
2 tablespoons flaked coconut
1 small (8 oz.) can orange segments in unsweetened juice

Beat together butter (or shortening), eggs, orange extract, and lemon juice until blended. Add juice concentrate and beat thoroughly. Measure in flour, baking soda, and baking powder. Beat well. Spoon batter into an oiled and floured 9″ square pan. Bake in a preheated oven at 325 degrees for 20 minutes or until firm to the touch. Do not remove cake from the pan. Cool on a wire rack to room temperature.

To prepare topping, mix together pineapple juice and cornstarch in a small saucepan. Cook over medium heat, stirring constantly, and bring to a boil. Boil 1 minute. Remove from the heat and cool to room temperature. Pour cooled pineapple mixture over cake, which is still in pan. Sprinkle with coconut and garnish with well-drained orange segments. Refrigerate until firm. To serve, cut into squares.

Serves 6.

LADY FINGERS

Light, sweet strips of cake that make the simplest dessert a fancy one.

CAKE:
4 eggs, separated (room temperature)
1 teaspoon vanilla extract
¼ cup plus 1 tablespoon unsweetened frozen pineapple-orange juice concentrate, thawed

¾ cup unbleached white flour
¼ teaspoon baking soda
¼ teaspoon baking powder

Line a 10" by 15" jelly roll pan with buttered wax paper; set aside. Beat egg yolks in a small bowl at high speed for 5 minutes or until thick and lemon colored. Add vanilla extract and pineapple-orange juice concentrate. Beat just to blend. Toss together flour, baking soda, and baking powder; fold into liquid. Set aside.

In a separate bowl beat egg whites until very thick and peaks hold their shape. Gently fold juice mixture into egg whites just until blended. Spoon batter into jelly roll pan, and smooth evenly in pan. Bake in a preheated oven at 325 degrees for 15 minutes or until firm to the touch. Allow cake to cool in the pan 10 minutes. With a sharp knife loosen cake from pan and pry up wax paper to loosen all edges. Cover cake with a large wire rack and flip over. Remove pan and carefully peel off wax paper. Use a sharp knife, if necessary, to loosen paper from cake. Allow to cool completely.

To make lady fingers, invert cooled cake onto a flat surface. Using a ruler as a guide cut cake into quarters lengthwise and 1" pieces widthwise. (See illustration.) Cut a small point on the end of each cake rectangle. Place lady fingers browned side down onto a large baking sheet. Bake in a preheated oven at 325 degrees for 5 minutes until crisp. Cool on wire racks.

Use as directed in recipes or freeze for future use. To freeze,

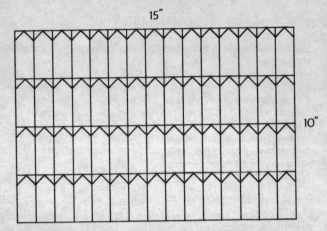

Slice cake into Lady Fingers as illustrated

loosely pack lady fingers in freezer containers. To use after freezing, place frozen lady fingers on baking sheets to thaw. Bake for 3 to 5 minutes in a 325 degree oven to crispness.

Yields 60.

PINEAPPLE UPSIDE-DOWN CAKES

Warm, individual minicakes topped with a pineapple ring and spicy syrup.

SYRUP:
1 8-oz. can sliced pineapple rings in unsweetened juice
1 tablespoon unsweetened frozen pineapple juice concentrate, thawed
½ teaspoon cornstarch
¼ teaspoon cinnamon or nutmeg
2 tablespoons butter (optional)

CAKE:
¼ cup butter, softened (or shortening)
1 large egg
1 teaspoon vanilla extract
½ cup unsweetened pineapple juice
1 cup unbleached white flour
½ teaspoon baking soda
½ teaspoon baking powder

To prepare syrup, drain juice from can of sliced pineapple into a small saucepan. Reserve the pineapple slices for use later. Add pineapple juice concentrate, spices, and cornstarch to saucepan. Mix well. While stirring constantly, bring to a boil over medium heat. Boil 1 minute. Remove from heat, stir in butter, and set aside.

To prepare cake, beat together butter (or shortening) and egg until creamy. Add vanilla extract and pineapple juice; beat thoroughly. Measure in flour, baking soda, and baking powder. Beat just until blended. Batter will be thick. Set aside.

Lightly butter 4 glass pyrex baking dishes approximately 4" in diameter. Spoon 1 tablespoon of syrup and place 1 ring of sliced pineapple into each dish. Top with batter, dividing it evenly in dishes. Spread to smooth. Bake in a preheated oven at 325 degrees for 25 to 30 minutes or until lightly browned. Remove from the oven. With a sharp knife loosen cake from baking dishes. Allow to cool 10 minutes, and turn out upside-down onto individual dessert saucers. Serve immediately.

Serves 4.

SENSATIONAL STRAWBERRY CAKE

A delicious sponge cake smothered with fluffy cream cheese and topped with sweet strawberries and syrup.

CAKE:
5 eggs, separated (room temperature)
¼ teaspoon almond extract
3 tablespoons unsweetened frozen pineapple or orange juice concentrate, thawed
1 tablespoon vanilla extract
¼ cup water

1 cup unbleached white flour
¼ teaspoon baking soda
¾ teaspoon cream of tartar

TOPPING:
Cream Cheese Filling (see page 108)
Strawberry Topping (see page 103)

Beat together egg yolks, almond extract, pineapple (or orange) juice concentrate, vanilla extract, and water for 2 to 3 minutes, or until light and fluffy. Toss together flour and baking soda in a small bowl; fold into egg yolk mixture.

Beat egg whites and cream of tartar until peaks form and hold their shape; mixture will be quite firm. Fold together with egg yolk mixture. Spoon batter into an ungreased 9" springform pan. Cut into batter with a knife to release any air bubbles. Smooth batter in pan. Bake in a preheated oven at 325 degrees for 50 minutes or until well browned. Turn pan upside-down over rack and allow to cool completely.

Prepare Cream Cheese Filling and Strawberry Topping as directed. Loosen cake from pan sides with a sharp knife; remove sides. Loosen cake from metal pan bottom with a sharp knife; remove bottom. Place cake upside-down on serving dish. Top generously with Cream Cheese Filling, using a pastry tube, if available. Spoon Strawberry Topping in the center. Refrigerate until serving.

Serves 8 to 10.

CHRISTMAS YULE LOG

Soft, sweet cake rolled with pure whipped cream and iced with cocoa. A favorite all year long.

CAKE:
5 large eggs, separated (room temperature)
4 tablespoons unsweetened orange juice
4 tablespoons unsweetened frozen orange juice concentrate, thawed
1 teaspoon vanilla extract
1 tablespoon lemon juice
¾ cup plus 2 tablespoons unbleached white flour

2 tablespoons unsweetened cocoa or carob powder
1 teaspoon cream of tartar

FILLING:
Creamy Topping (see page 104)

ICING:
Chocolate Icing (see page 110)

To prepare cake, beat egg yolks at high speed in a small bowl for 5 minutes; mixture will be thick and lemon colored. In a separate bowl combine orange juice, orange juice concentrate, vanilla extract, and lemon juice. In another bowl toss together flour and cocoa (or carob). Alternately add orange juice mixture and flour mixture to egg yolks, beating well after each addition. Set aside.

In a large bowl, and with clean beaters, beat egg whites until foamy. Add cream of tartar and beat until firm and stiff. Do not underbeat. Gently fold liquid orange mixture into egg whites until blended. Spoon mixture into a foil-lined large jelly roll pan, approximately 12" by 18" or slightly larger. Spread batter evenly in pan. Bake in a preheated oven at 325 degrees for 10 minutes or until firm. Cool in the pan 5 minutes. Loosen cake edges from pan with a sharp knife. Cover pan with a clean kitchen towel, and flip cake out onto the counter. Remove pan and gently peel off foil. Loosely roll cake and towel around an empty paper towel or plastic wrap cardboard tube, starting at the narrow end. Cool on a wire rack 20 minutes. Very slowly and carefully unroll cake, remove towel, and reroll. Cool.

Prepare Creamy Topping as directed. Gently unroll cake, spread with cream, and reroll. Place seam side down on a serving platter.

Prepare Chocolate Icing as directed. Spoon over cake. Store refrigerated until serving. May be garnished with Fancy Touches (see page 115).

Serves 6.

BONNIE BLACKBERRY SHORTCAKE

A large dessert biscuit filled and topped with sweet berries and cream.

FILLING:
Ritz Blackberry Pudding (see page 26)

BISCUIT:
2 cups unbleached white flour
2 teaspoons baking powder

¼ cup chilled butter (or shortening)
¾ cup milk
2 tablespoons melted butter

TOPPING:
Creamy Topping (see page 104)

Prepare Ritz Blackberry Pudding as directed; store refrigerated.

Mix together flour, baking powder, and butter (or shortening) until evenly blended. Stir in milk. Divide batter in half. Roll each into a ball, flatten, and roll out on a floured surface to a 9″ circle. Place one circle in a buttered 9″ cake pan, brush with melted butter, and cover with remaining circle. Bake in a preheated oven at 425 degrees for 10 to 12 minutes or until just lightly browned. While baking, prepare Creamy Topping as directed.

Remove shortcake from the oven, cover with a wire rack and invert. Cover with serving dish and invert again. Slide an edgeless cookie sheet between circles or use spatulas to gently remove top biscuit. Spread liberally with Ritz Blackberry Pudding and top with biscuit, more pudding, and whipped topping. Serve immediately, cutting into pie-shaped wedges.

Serves 6.

STRAWBERRY SHORTCAKES

Tasty little shortcakes filled with sweet strawberries and topped with cream.

FILLING:
3 cups fresh strawberries, hulled
   and sliced
Unsweetened frozen pineapple
   juice concentrate, thawed

3 teaspoons baking powder
⅓ cup chilled butter (or shortening)
½ teaspoon vanilla extract
⅔ to ¾ cup milk

BISCUITS:
2 cups unbleached white flour

TOPPING:
Creamy Topping (see page 104)

Place sliced strawberries in a bowl. Sweeten with pineapple juice concentrate to taste. Crush gently with the back of a spoon. Refrigerate.

To prepare biscuits, mix together flour, baking powder, and butter until evenly blended. Add vanilla extract. Gradually add milk, adding just enough to form a soft dough. Roll dough out on a floured surface to ½″ thickness. Cut into 12 3″-rounds, and place on buttered baking sheet. Bake in a preheated oven at 425 degrees for 12 minutes or until just lightly browned. While baking, prepare Creamy Topping as directed. Store refrigerated.

Slice warm biscuits in half horizontally. Place each bottom half in a dessert saucer, spoon over strawberry mixture, and top with remaining biscuit half, more strawberries, and topping. Serve immediately.

Serves 6.

• *Note:* You'll find some additional recipes for cakes, with delicious gelatin fillings, in the Gelatin Desserts chapter.

Cheesecakes

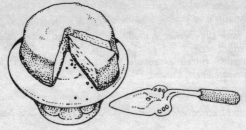

FANCY FLUFF CHEESECAKE

A light and sweet combination of cream, pineapple, and cream cheese with just a touch of vanilla. Literally melts in your mouth!

PASTRY:
1 cup unsweetened granola (see page 129 to prepare your own)
2 tablespoons melted butter

FILLING:
2 tablespoons unflavored gelatin (2 packets)
½ cup cold water
1 20-oz. can crushed pineapple in unsweetened juice

2 8-oz. packages cream cheese, softened
1 tablespoon vanilla extract
Creamy Topping (see page 104)

TOPPING:
Cream Rosettes (see page 106)
1 small (8-oz.) can tangerine segments in unsweetened juice
Mint leaves (optional)

Whip granola in a blender or food processor until finely ground; or place granola in a plastic bag and repeatedly crush with a rolling pin. Toss with melted butter and press evenly in the bottom of a 9" spring-form pan. Bake in a preheated oven at 375 degrees for 10 minutes or until lightly browned. Cool and refrigerate.

In a small bowl sprinkle gelatin over cold water and allow to set 5 minutes to soften. Place bowl containing softened gelatin over another filled with hot water (like a double boiler), and set aside while gelatin dissolves into a clear liquid. If hot water cools before gelatin has dissolved, discard and replace with more hot water. If you prefer, gelatin may be dissolved in a small saucepan over low heat. Meanwhile, whip crushed pineapple, including juice, in a blender until smooth. Add cream cheese and vanilla. Whip until smooth. Pour in dissolved gelatin and whip just to mix. Pour mixture into a bowl and refrigerate a short while until thickened, but not set. Remove from the refrigerator and beat briefly. Prepare Creamy Topping as directed. Fold into gelatin mixture. Spoon into spring-form pan. Refrigerate to set, overnight if possible.

Before serving, loosen cake from pan edges with a sharp knife. Remove pan sides. Slide cake, metal bottom attached, onto serving plate. Garnish cheesecake with Cream Rosettes (as directed on page 106), well-drained tangerine segments, and mint leaves.

Serves 10 to 12.

CHOCOLATE SWIRL CHEESECAKE

Sweetened with banana and packed full of nutritious cheese, this double-layer cheesecake is a favorite with chocolate lovers.

PASTRY:
1 cup unsweetened granola (see
    page 129 to prepare your own)
1 tablespoon unsweetened cocoa
    or carob powder
2 tablespoons melted butter

FILLING:
2 tablespoons unflavored gelatin
    (2 packets)
½ cup cold water
1 cup mashed banana (mash ripe
    banana with a fork)
2 8-oz. packages cream cheese,
    softened

1 cup cottage cheese
2 teaspoons vanilla extract
Creamy Topping (see page 104)
3 tablespoons unsweetened cocoa
    or carob powder
4 unbeaten egg whites, room tem-
    perature

TOPPING:
Chocolate Glaze (see page 110)
Cream Cheese Rosettes (see
    page 108)

To prepare pastry, whip granola in a blender or food processor until finely ground, or place in a plastic bag and repeatedly crush with a rolling pin until ground. Mix with melted butter, and pat evenly in the bottom of a 9″ springform pan. Bake in a preheated oven at 375 degrees for 10 minutes. Cool and refrigerate.

Soften gelatin in a small bowl with cold water for 5 minutes. Place bowl of softened gelatin over another filled with hot water (like a double boiler), and allow to set until gelatin dissolves into a clear liquid. If hot water cools before gelatin has dissolved, discard and replace with more hot water. If you prefer, gelatin may be dissolved in a small saucepan over low heat.

Meanwhile, beat together mashed banana and cream cheese until creamy. Add cottage cheese and beat until smooth. Add vanilla extract. Gradually stir in Creamy Topping. Divide mixture evenly into 2 bowls, approximately 2½ cups per bowl. To one bowl add cocoa or carob powder; mix on low speed just until blended. Beat egg whites until stiff peaks form and set aside. Pour half of the dissolved gelatin mixture (¼ cup) into the cocoa mixture. Beat on low speed just until mixed. Fold in half of the beaten egg whites. Spread mixture evenly in pastry-lined springform pan. Pour remaining gelatin into remaining filling, and beat on low speed just until mixed. Fold in beaten egg whites. Spoon gently over cocoa mixture; smooth in pan. Refrigerate to set.

Prepare Chocolate Glaze as directed. Drop by spoonfuls in a spiral pattern over cake. Refrigerate cake at least several hours to set. Before serving, run a sharp knife between cake and pan sides. Gently remove sides. Slide cake, pan bottom attached, onto serving dish. Garnish top edge of cake with Cream Cheese Rosettes prepared as directed.

Serves 10 to 12.

BLUEBERRY CHEESECAKES

Rich pastry shells filled with lemony cream-cheese filling and topped with fresh blueberries.

PASTRY:
½ cup butter, softened
1 3-oz. package cream cheese, softened
1¼ cups unbleached white flour

FILLING:
2 8-oz. packages cream cheese, softened

1 teaspoon lemon juice
2 teaspoons vanilla extract
¼ teaspoon lemon extract
½ cup milk

TOPPING:
1 cup fresh blueberries, approximately

To prepare pastry, cream together butter and cream cheese. Gradually add flour and mix until blended. Refrigerate dough a short while, if sticky. Pinch off pieces of dough and press evenly into medium-sized muffin wells, covering the bottom and sides. Do not use paper or foil muffin liners. Refrigerate pastries until firm. Prick well with a fork. Bake in a preheated oven at 400 degrees for 5 minutes. Remove from the oven and prick any pastries that have puffed with a fork. Return to the oven to bake an additional 5 minutes or until lightly browned around the edges. Cool 10 minutes in the pans. Remove carefully to cool on wire racks.

Combine all filling ingredients and beat until thoroughly blended. Spoon generously into pastry shells, and refrigerate to set. Completely cover the top of each minicheesecake with fresh blueberries, top side up. Store refrigerated.

Yields 10 to 12 cheesecakes.

VENETIAN RICOTTA SQUARES

Cheesecake bars generously topped with raspberries.

TOPING:
Ritz Raspberry Pudding (see page 25)

SQUARES:
3 cups (1½ pounds) ricotta cheese
3 eggs

1 tablespoon vanilla extract
½ teaspoon almond extract
¼ teaspoon lemon extract
1 teaspoon lemon juice

GARNISH:
Cream Rosettes (see page 106)

Prepare Ritz Raspberry Pudding as directed; set aside.

To prepare squares, beat together all the ingredients until well blended. Pour into an oiled and floured 9″ square baking pan. Smooth batter evenly in pan. Bake in a preheated oven at 350 degrees for 50 minutes or until a knife inserted comes out clean. Cool and refrigerate in pan until chilled. Spread topping over cheese filling to within ¼″ of edge. Squares will have formed a raised edge while cooling. Refrigerate to set.

To serve, cut into squares, and remove from the pan with a spatula. Place attractively on serving dish or on individual plates. May be garnished with Cream Rosettes, if desired.

Serves 6 to 9.

PINEAPPLE CREAM CHEESE PIE

A rich cream-cheese filling is poured into a sweet pastry crust and topped with pineapple and coconut.

PASTRY:

1¼ cups unbleached white flour
¼ cup chilled butter (or shortening)
6 tablespoons unsweetened pineapple juice, approximately

FILLING:

1 8-oz. package cream cheese, softened
2 large eggs, separated (room temperature)

2 cups sour cream or plain yogurt
3 tablespoons unbleached white flour
2 teaspoons vanilla extract

TOPPING:

1 20-oz. can crushed pineapple in unsweetened juice
2 tablespoons cornstarch
2 tablespoons flaked coconut

Mix together flour and butter (or shortening) until crumbly. Gradually add pineapple juice, using just enough to form a soft dough. Roll out on a lightly floured surface to ⅛" thickness. Fit pastry into a 9" pie pan, trim off excess, and flute edges. Prick pastry with a fork. Bake in a preheated oven at 425 degrees for 5 to 10 minutes or until lightly browned. Cool and refrigerate.

To prepare filling, beat together cream cheese and egg yolks, reserving whites to use later, until creamy. Add sour cream and flour; beat well. Cook mixture in the top of a double boiler set over simmering water. Stir constantly until mixture thickens, about 10 minutes. Remove from the heat and cool to room temperature. Beat in vanilla extract. In a small bowl beat egg whites until firm peaks form, and fold into cream cheese mixture. Spoon filling into pastry-lined pie pan. Refrigerate until firm.

Meanwhile, prepare topping. Empty the can of crushed pineapple into a strainer, catching the liquid in a bowl. Press pineapple bits with the back of a spoon to squeeze out juice. Combine juice with cornstarch and mix well. Cook, stirring constantly, over medium heat until mixture thickens. Cool and mix in crushed pineapple pieces. Refrigerate. After cheese filling has set, gently cover with pineapple topping and sprinkle with flaked coconut. Store refrigerated.

Serves 6 to 8.

Custards, Puddings, and Compotes

PEACH CUSTARD CASSEROLE

Sweet peaches and light custard combine in a pastry-lined casserole.

PASTRY:
1 cup unbleached white flour
½ cup butter (or shortening)
2 tablespoons yogurt (or sour cream)

FILLING:
1 29-oz. can sliced peaches in unsweetened juice (or 3 cups sliced fresh peaches)

CUSTARD:
1 cup milk
3 egg yolks
3 tablespoons unbleached white flour
1 teaspoon vanilla extract

TOPPING:
Nutmeg

Blend together flour and butter (or shortening) until evenly mixed. Add yogurt and mix well. Press pastry evenly on the bottom and up the sides of an 8" by 8" baking casserole. Line the pastry evenly with well-drained peaches (or peaches sliced fresh). Whip custard ingredients together in a blender or mix with a beater. Pour over peaches. Sprinkle generously with nutmeg. Bake casserole in a preheated oven at 400 degrees for 5 minutes, turn heat to 350 degrees, and continue baking for 50 more minutes or until custard has set. Cool and refrigerate.

Serves 6.

HEAVENLY COCOA MOUSSE

A light and fluffy dessert full of cocoa, sweet banana, and cream.

MOUSSE:
1 tablespoon unflavored gelatin (1 packet)
¼ cup cold water
2 cups mashed banana (mash ripe banana with a fork)
1 teaspoon lemon juice
1 tablespoon vanilla extract
1 tablespoon unsweetened cocoa or carob powder
Creamy Topping (see page 104)

Sprinkle gelatin over cold water in a small bowl; allow to set 5 minutes to soften. Place bowl containing softened gelatin over another filled with hot water (like a double boiler), and set aside while gelatin dissolves into a clear liquid. If hot water cools before gelatin has dissolved, discard and replace with more hot water. If you prefer, gelatin may be dissolved in a small saucepan over low heat. Meanwhile, beat mashed banana, lemon juice, vanilla extract, and cocoa until light and fluffy, beating at least 3 minutes at high speed. Add dissolved gelatin, and beat until evenly blended. Refrigerate mixture until it reaches a consistency slightly thicker than unbeaten egg white. In a small bowl prepare Creamy Topping as directed. Fold into cocoa mixture. Refrigerate to set. To serve, spoon into individual dessert goblets. May be garnished as desired.

Serves 4 to 6.

IN-A-JIFFY RICE PUDDING

Turn your leftover rice into a tasty, sweet, and nutritious dessert.

PUDDING:
2 cups cooked rice
1 16-oz. can crushed pineapple
   in unsweetened juice, well
   drained
1 teaspoon vanilla extract
½ recipe Creamy Topping (see
   page 104)

TOPPING:
3 tablespoons flaked coconut
1 small (8-oz.) can of chunk pineapple in unsweetened juice,
   well drained
Mint leaves (optional)

Prepare Creamy Topping as directed. Combine all pudding ingredients and mix well. Chill. To serve, spoon ½ cup into each
dessert goblet and top with a teaspoon of flaked coconut, chunk of
pineapple, and colorful mint leaf.

Serves 8.

RITZ RASPBERRY PUDDING

Serve this tasty purple pudding in light meringue shells as an attractive and formal dessert.

PASTRY:
Meringue Shells (see page 63)

PUDDING:
1 10-oz. package unsweetened
   frozen whole raspberries,
   thawed
⅓ cup unsweetened frozen
   pineapple juice concentrate,
   thawed

1 teaspoon lemon juice
3 tablespoons cornstarch
1 cup mashed banana (mash ripe
   banana with a fork)
½ teaspoon vanilla extract

TOPPING:
½ recipe Creamy Topping (see
   page 104)

Prepare Meringue Shells as directed. Purée and sieve raspberries. (Whip berries briefly in a blender and press through a fine strainer, screening out seeds. Discard seeds.) Beat together puréed raspberries, pineapple juice concentrate, lemon juice, cornstarch, and mashed banana until well blended. (Mixture may be whipped in a blender.) Pour mixture into a saucepan and, stirring constantly, bring to a boil over medium heat. Boil 1 minute. Mixture will thicken. Cool. Stir in vanilla extract. Refrigerate until well chilled.

Prepare Creamy Topping as directed. To serve, spoon pudding generously into Meringue Shells, and top each with a dollop of topping. Serve immediately.

Serves 6.

•Variations

Ritz Blackberry Pudding: Prepare as directed above, substituting frozen blackberries for frozen raspberries.

Strawberry Pudding: Prepare as directed above, substituting frozen strawberries for frozen raspberries; increase cornstarch to ¼ cup. Natural red food coloring may be added to deepen the color.

APPLE RICE PUDDING

A warm rice pudding filled with dates, raisins, apple, and topped with a spicy apple syrup.

PUDDING:
2 cups cooked rice
½ cup chopped dates
½ cup raisins
1 beaten egg
¾ cup milk
1 teaspoon vanilla extract

¼ teaspoon cinnamon
1 cup chopped apple
¼ teaspoon nutmeg

TOPPING:
Spicy Apple Glaze (see page 110)

Combine pudding ingredients in a 1½ quart baking casserole. Mix well. Bake in a preheated oven at 350 degrees for 30 minutes or until browned. Meanwhile, prepare Spicy Apple Glaze as directed. Spoon warm casserole out into individual dessert bowls, and top with glaze.

Serves 6.

ORANGE MARSHMALLOW TAPIOCA

Orange juice, tapioca, egg whites, and flavorings all combine to make a light, flavorful dessert.

TAPIOCA:
2 cups unsweetened orange juice
2 tablespoons quick cooking tapioca
1 small (11-oz.) can orange segments in unsweetened juice, well drained (optional)

2 teaspoons vanilla extract
¼ teaspoon orange extract
2 egg whites, room temperature
¼ teaspoon cream of tartar

Combine orange juice, tapioca, and well-drained orange segments in a saucepan. Allow to set 5 minutes. Bring to a boil over medium heat and, stirring constantly, boil 5 minutes. Meanwhile, whip egg whites and cream of tartar until peaks form and hold their shape; set aside. Stir extracts into cooked tapioca. Fold in whipped egg whites. Cool for 20 minutes. Stir thoroughly. Refrigerate until well chilled. To serve, spoon into individual dessert goblets. May be garnished as desired.

Serves 6 to 8.

BLACKBERRY TAPIOCA

A deep purple pudding with a delightful sweet-sour flavor.

PUDDING:
1 12-oz. package unsweetened
  frozen whole blackberries,
  thawed

½ cup unsweetened frozen
  pineapple juice concentrate,
  thawed
2 tablespoons quick-cooking
  tapioca

   Purée and sieve blackberries. (Whip berries briefly in a blender
and press through a fine strainer, screening out seeds. Discard seeds.)
Combine ingredients in a small saucepan and allow to set 5 minutes.
Stirring constantly, bring to a boil over medium heat. Boil 1 minute.
Remove from the heat and cool 20 minutes. Stir well. Spoon into
a bowl and refrigerate until thoroughly chilled. To serve, spoon into
individual dessert goblets.

Serves 4.

•Variation

Raspberry Tapioca: Prepare as directed above, substituting frozen
raspberries for blackberries.

PEARS À LA RASPBERRIES

A delicious chilled compote of pears smothered with raspberry sauce.

PEARS:
8 fresh pears

SAUCE:
1 10-oz. package frozen whole
  raspberries, thawed
⅓ cup unsweetened frozen
  pineapple juice concentrate,
  thawed

1 teaspoon lemon juice
2 tablespoons cornstarch
2 tablespoons cold water
1 cup mashed banana (mash ripe
  banana with a fork)
½ teaspoon vanilla extract

Leaving stems attached, peel pears, and slice a thin layer of fruit off the bottom so pears will stand upright. Place standing up in a heavy saucepan.

Purée and sieve raspberries to remove seeds. (Whip berries briefly in a blender and press through a fine strainer, screening out seeds. Discard seeds.) Whip together raspberries (including juice), pineapple concentrate, and lemon juice in a blender. Pour over pears. Lift up each pear slightly to allow juice to cover pan bottom. Bring to a boil, turn to low, cover, and simmer over low heat until tender, about 20 minutes. Baste pears occasionally as they cook. Remove pears from pan, cool, and store refrigerated. Combine cornstarch with water in a small bowl; mix well. Add to raspberry mixture. Stirring constantly, bring to a boil; boil 1 minute. Remove thickened liquid and cool. Beat in mashed banana and vanilla extract. Store refrigerated. To serve, place each pear in an individual dessert saucer. Spoon over raspberry topping, about ¼ cup per pear. May be garnished with whipped cream or fresh fruit, as desired.

Serves 8.

Cookies and Turnovers

DATE SQUARES

Very sweet and rich cookie squares.

TOPPING:
1 cup chopped dates, pits removed
¾ cup water

PASTRY:
1 cup unbleached white flour
6 tablespoons chilled butter (see note below)

Combine dates and water in a small saucepan. Bring to a boil, turn to low, and simmer, covered, for 10 minutes. Remove from the heat. Mash date mixture until smooth.

Meanwhile, mix together flour and butter until crumbly. Sprinkle mixture evenly in an 8" by 8" baking pan. Press mixture firmly in pan. Bake in a preheated oven at 350 degrees for 15 minutes. Remove from the oven, spread evenly with mashed dates, and bake 15 additional minutes. Cool in the pan. With a sharp knife cut into 1" squares.

Yields 16 small squares.

• *Note:* Shortening is not recommended in this recipe.

FANCY CHEESECAKE BARS

Sweet cream cheese bars with a spicy bottom crust and sweet strawberry topping.

PASTRY:
½ cup finely chopped walnuts
   (whip in a food processor or
   blender)
1 cup unbleached white flour
⅓ cup butter, softened
1 teaspoon cinnamon
1 cup raisins or chopped dates,
   pits removed

FILLING:
2 8-oz. packages of cream cheese,
   softened
⅓ cup mashed banana (mash
   ripe banana with a fork)

2 large eggs
¼ cup milk
2 teaspoons vanilla extract

TOPPING:
1 12-oz. package of frozen whole
   strawberries (loose pack and
   sugarfree), thawed
2 tablespoons unsweetened frozen pineapple juice concentrate, thawed
2 tablespoons cornstarch

GARNISH:
Creamy Frosting (see page 105)

In a medium-sized bowl mix together pastry ingredients until light and crumbly. Press firmly and evenly in a 9″ by 13″ ungreased baking pan. Bake in a preheated oven at 350 degrees for 15 minutes.

Meanwhile, beat together all filling ingredients until smooth. Spoon evenly over baked pastry, and bake for an additional 20 to 25 minutes or until a knife inserted comes out clean. Cool on a wire rack.

To prepare topping whip together ingredients in a blender until smooth and creamy. Bring to a boil over medium heat, stirring constantly. Boil 1 minute. Remove from heat and pour over cheesecake. Spread until evenly covered with a thin layer of topping. Cool and refrigerate until thoroughly chilled. To serve, cut into bars. Bars may be decorated with Creamy Frosting pressed through a cake decorating tube. See Cake Decorating, page 121, for suggestions.

Yields 24 bars.

REFRIGERATOR GRANOLA BARS

Unusual bars filled with granola, dried fruit, and crushed pineapple.

BARS:
3 tablespoons unflavored gelatin
   (3 packets)
¾ cup cold water
1 20-oz. can crushed pineapple in
   unsweetened juice
2 cups unsweetened granola (see
   page 129 to prepare your own)

1 cup raisins or chopped dates,
   pits removed
1 cup flaked coconut

TOPPING:
¼ cup flaked coconut

Sprinkle gelatin over cold water in a small bowl; allow to set 5 minutes to soften. Place bowl containing softened gelatin over a bowl filled with hot water (like a double boiler); set aside while gelatin dissolves into a clear liquid. If hot water cools before gelatin has dissolved, discard and replace with more hot water. If you prefer, gelatin may be dissolved in a small saucepan over low heat. Meanwhile, mix together remaining bar ingredients. Beat in dissolved gelatin.

Spread mixture evenly in an ungreased 9″ by 13″ baking pan. Sprinkle with ¼ cup flaked coconut. Refrigerate until firm. To serve, cut into bars.

Yields 24 bars.

FIG BARS

Two layers of rich pastry filled with a sweet fig spread.

PASTRY:
3 cups unbleached white flour
1 cup butter or shortening
8 tablespoons cold water, approximately

FILLING:
1 cup firmly packed chopped dried figs
1 cup water
1 teaspoon lemon juice
1 teaspoon vanilla extract

Using your fingers, mix together butter (or shortening) and flour until crumbly. Gradually add water, adding just enough to form a soft dough; mix well. Divide pastry in half, roll each into a ball, and flatten to form a square. Wrap in plastic wrap and refrigerate until firm.

To prepare filling, combine chopped figs, water, and lemon juice in a small saucepan. Bring to a boil, cover, and simmer on low heat 30 minutes. Cool, and stir in vanilla extract. Whip mixture in a food processor or with an electric mixer until creamy. Store refrigerated.

Roll out 1 square of chilled pastry to an 8" by 12" rectangle on a generously floured surface. Place pastry on an ungreased baking sheet, preferably without edges. Spread fig filling evenly over pastry, stopping ⅛" in from the pastry edges. Roll out second pastry square as the first, and gently place over filling. With the tines of a fork carefully crimp edges together to seal in filling. With a sharp knife cut a few air vents in the top crust.

Bake in a preheated oven at 400 degrees for 30 minutes. Cool 10 minutes on the baking sheet. With spatulas, transfer pastry to a wire rack to cool. Using a sharp knife, cut cooled pastry with a sawing motion into 2" squares. Store refrigerated.

Yields 24 squares.

DATE SANDWICH COOKIES

Large, round sandwich cookies with a sweet date filling.

PASTRY:
1 cup unbleached white flour
⅓ cup butter (or shortening)
½ teaspoon baking soda
2 to 3 tablespoons chilled un-
  sweetened pineapple juice

FILLING:
1 cup firmly packed chopped
  dates, pits discarded
1 cup water

Mix together flour and butter (or shortening). Add baking soda. Gradually add fruit juice, using just enough to form a soft dough. Roll out on a floured surface to ⅛" thickness. Cut pastry into 3" rounds. Cut a 1" circle out of the centers of half the rounds. Place large solid rounds and rings on an ungreased baking sheet. Prick lightly with a fork. Bake in a preheated oven at 375 degrees for 4 to 5 minutes or until nicely browned. Carefully remove rounds to a wire rack to cool.

To prepare filling, combine chopped dates and water in a small saucepan. Bring to a boil, turn to low, and continue cooking, covered, for 10 minutes. Remove from the heat. Mash with a fork until smooth and creamy. Cool and refrigerate.

To assemble cookies, spoon chilled date filling onto solid pastry rounds, spreading evenly over rounds, and top with pastry rings. Handle cookies carefully, since the pastry is fragile. Store refrigerated.

Yields 12 large cookies.

STRAWBERRY JAM TURNOVERS

Flaky pastry filled with sweet strawberry.

FILLING:
2 cups Strawberry Jam (see page 112)

PASTRY:
2 cups unbleached white flour

⅔ cup chilled butter (see note below)
¼ teaspoon almond extract (optional)
5 to 6 tablespoons cold water, approximately

Prepare Strawberry Jam as directed; store refrigerated.

To make pastry, mix together flour, butter, and almond extract until blended. Gradually add water, adding just enough to form a soft dough. Divide in half, roll into balls, flatten, wrap in plastic wrap, and refrigerate until firm.

Roll pastry circles out one at a time on a floured surface to ⅛" thickness. Cut into 2½" rounds. Spoon 1 level teaspoon of strawberry filling into the center of half of the rounds, and spread almost to the edges. Slice a cross measuring 1¼" by 1¼" into each of the remaining pastry rounds.

To assemble, wet the edges of the filled rounds with water. Top with cross-sliced rounds. Secure edges together by pressing firmly with the tines of a fork. Place on an ungreased cookie sheet. Refrigerate until firm.

Bake in a preheated oven at 475 degrees for 8 to 10 minutes or until lightly browned. Cool on wire racks.

Yields approximately 60.

• *Note:* Shortening is not recommended in this recipe.

FLAKY APPLE TURNOVERS

Flaky turnovers filled with chopped apple, raisins, and dates, and topped with chocolate icing.

FILLING:
¼ cup raisins
¼ cup firmly packed chopped dates, pitted
¼ cup water
1½ cups finely diced apple (peel, core, and dice approximately 3 apples)
¼ teaspoon lemon juice
½ teaspoon cinnamon
¼ teaspoon nutmeg
2 tablespoons unsweetened applesauce

2 tablespoons unbleached white flour

PASTRY:
5 12" by 16" strudel pastry sheets (available in supermarket frozen food section)
3 tablespoons melted butter, approximately

TOPPING:
Chocolate Icing (see page 110)

Combine raisins, dates, and water in a small saucepan. Bring to a boil, turn heat to low, and cook, covered, 10 minutes. Mash with a fork until smooth. Allow to cool slightly. Meanwhile, toss together diced apple, lemon juice, spices, applesauce, and flour. Mix in raisin mixture. Set aside.

Thaw pastry as directed on package. Lay one pastry sheet out on a flat surface and brush with melted butter. Cover with additional sheets, brushing each with melted butter until all sheets are stacked. Using a ruler and sharp knife, cut through pastry sheets to form 12 4" by 4" squares.

Spoon about 1½ tablespoons of filling into the center of each square. Gently spread filling out slightly. Wet edges of pastry with water. Fold pastry over to form triangles, pressing down to secure seams. Prick top with a sharp knife. Place on ungreased baking sheets and brush tops with melted butter. Bake in a preheated oven at 375 degrees for 10 to 12 minutes or until just lightly browned. Cool on wire racks.

Prepare Chocolate Icing as directed and drizzle over turnovers. Serve warm or cooled.

Yields 12.

CREAM CHEESE AND DATE CRESCENTS

A very rich pastry dessert with sweet date filling.

FILLING:
½ cup firmly packed chopped dates, pits removed
¼ cup water

PASTRY:
3-oz. package cream cheese
2½ tablespoons butter
1 teaspoon vanilla extract
½ cup unbleached white flour

Combine filling ingredients in a small saucepan. Cover, bring to a boil, turn to low, and simmer 15 minutes. Remove from the heat, and mash mixture with a fork. Set aside to cool.

To make pastry, cream together cream cheese, butter, and vanilla extract. Gradually add flour and mix well. Roll into a ball, cover with plastic wrap, and refrigerate until firm.

Roll out a section of dough at a time on a floured surface to ⅛" thickness. Sprinkle the pastry with flour as needed to prevent sticking. Cut into 3" rounds. Place 1 teaspoon of filling in the center of each round. Wet the edges with water, fold in half, and press edges firmly together with the tines of a fork. Dip the fork in flour occasionally to prevent sticking. Place pastries on an ungreased baking sheet. Bake in a preheated oven at 400 degrees for 10 minutes. Cool on wire racks.

Yields 20 to 24 pastries.

Frozen Desserts

FROZEN PINEAPPLE CREAM PIE

Turn a can of crushed pineapple into a delicious frozen pineapple dessert.

PASTRY:
2 cups flaked coconut
¼ cup butter, softened (or shortening)

FILLING:
1 20-oz. can crushed pineapple in unsweetened juice

Double recipe Creamy Topping (see page 104)
2 tablespoons unsweetened frozen pineapple juice concentrate, thawed

Mix together flaked coconut and butter (or shortening). Pat mixture evenly on the bottom and up the sides of a large 10″ pie pan. (If a smaller-sized pan is substituted, extra filling can be frozen in freezer containers as ice cream.) Cover crust with a 9″ pie pan and press firmly to even out coconut crust. Remove smaller pie pan. Bake coconut crust in a preheated oven at 300 degrees for 15 to 20 minutes or until nicely browned. Cool and refrigerate.

To prepare filling, empty can of crushed pineapple, including

juice, into an 8" square pan. Freeze until top is frozen, but bottom
layer still soft. Whip together creamy topping and pineapple juice
concentrate just until peaks form and hold their shape. Set aside.

Whip partially frozen pineapple mixture in a bowl until it breaks
apart into pieces. Add to cream mixture and beat on low speed just
until mixture is thick enough to hold its shape if spooned into a
mound. Spoon filling into coconut crust, piling it up in the center.
If mixture does not hold its shape, beat slightly longer. Freeze until
firm, then place pie in refrigerator to soften, at least 30 to 45 minutes
before serving.

Serves 8 to 10.

APPLE-BANANA FREEZE

A double-layer frozen dessert filled with sweet apple concentrate,
buttermilk, creamy topping, and sliced banana—sure to be a taste-
pleaser!

FIRST LAYER:
1 tablespoon unflavored gelatin
   (1 packet)
¼ cup cold water
1 cup unsweetened frozen apple
   juice concentrate, thawed

1 cup buttermilk

SECOND LAYER:
2 egg whites, room temperature
Creamy Topping (see page 104)
1½ cups banana, thinly sliced

Sprinkle gelatin over cold water in a small bowl, and allow to set
5 minutes to soften. Place bowl containing softened gelatin over
another filled with hot water (like a double boiler) and set aside to
dissolve into a clear liquid. If hot water cools before gelatin has
dissolved, discard and replace with more hot water. If you prefer,
gelatin may be dissolved in a small saucepan over low heat. Warm
apple juice concentrate in a small saucepan to lukewarm. Remove
from the heat, and stir in dissolved gelatin. Stir constantly while
slowly adding buttermilk. Pour into a bowl. Freeze just until mixture
gels, then remove from the freezer and whip at high speed until

mixture is smooth. Pour into a 6-cup dessert mold and freeze again.

To prepare second layer, whip egg whites in a small bowl until peaks form and hold their shape; set aside. Prepare Creamy Topping as directed. Fold together egg whites, Creamy Topping, and thinly sliced banana. Spread evenly over first layer in dessert mold. Return to the freezer and freeze until solid.

To serve, allow mold to soften in the refrigerator 30 minutes. Turn out onto serving dish. May be garnished with additional whipped cream, sliced banana, or fresh apple.

Serves 6 to 8.

BANANA SHERBET

A delicious banana cream sherbet.

SHERBET:
½ cup mashed banana (mash ripe banana with a fork)
½ cup unsweetened frozen orange juice concentrate, thawed
1 cup milk

Creamy Topping (see page 104)
4 egg whites, room temperature

GARNISH:
Sliced fresh banana

Beat mashed banana with a mixer until light and fluffy. Add orange juice concentrate and milk. Beat at high speed at least 2 minutes. Pour mixture into an 8" square baking pan. Freeze until firm but not frozen solid, occasionally stirring mixture so it will freeze evenly.

Prepare Creamy Topping as directed; set aside. Beat egg whites until light and fluffy; set aside. Remove partially frozen mixture from the freezer and beat just until smooth. Fold in Creamy Topping and egg whites. Spoon mixture into a 6-cup mold or freezer container, and freeze until firm.

Allow mixture to thaw in the refrigerator at least 30 minutes before serving. Sherbet may be garnished with sliced banana.

Serves 6 to 8.

BLUEBERRY MOUSSE

An easy, creamy mousse speckled with bits of tasty blueberries.

MOUSSE:
2 egg whites, room temperature
Creamy Topping (see page 104)
1 teaspoon vanilla extract
1 tablespoon unsweetened frozen
    pineapple juice concentrate,
    thawed

¾ cup frozen blueberries, loose
    pack and sugarfree (see note
    below)

SAUCE:
Blueberry Sauce (see page 102)

Whip egg whites until stiff; set aside. Prepare Creamy Topping as directed. Beat in vanilla extract. In a food processor or blender whip frozen blueberries until finely ground to the consistency of snow. Combine all ingredients, including pineapple juice concentrate, and quickly fold together with a spatula just until evenly mixed. Spoon into a 4-cup mold, cover, and freeze.

Prepare Blueberry Sauce as directed; store refrigerated. Allow frozen mousse to soften slightly at room temperature before unmolding onto serving dish. Spoon mousse into dessert saucers and top generously with Blueberry Sauce. Serve immediately.

Serves 4.

• *Note:* If frozen blueberries are not available, fresh blueberries may be substituted. Place single layer of fresh berries on a cookie sheet and freeze. Use as directed above.

TANGY GRAPE SHERBET

An icy purple sherbet full of flavorful grape juice. A real treat for kids.

SHERBET:
1 teaspoon unflavored gelatin
1 tablespoon cold water
1¼ cups unsweetened pineapple
    juice

1¼ cups unsweetened grape
    juice
1 large egg white, room tempera-
    ture
½ recipe Creamy Topping (see
    page 104)

In a small bowl sprinkle gelatin over cold water; allow to set 5 minutes to soften. Place bowl containing softened gelatin over another filled with hot water (like a double boiler) and set aside while gelatin dissolves into a clear liquid. If hot water cools before gelatin has dissolved, discard and replace with more hot water. If you prefer, gelatin may be dissolved in a small saucepan over low heat.

If using fresh or frozen pineapple juice, it must be boiled for 3 minutes to destroy an enzyme that interferes with proper gelation. Canned pineapple juice need not be boiled.

Combine juices with dissolved gelatin and mix well. Pour mixture into a 9″ square pan and freeze. Stir occasionally as mixture freezes so it will form a uniform slushy consistency.

In a small bowl beat egg white until stiff; set aside. In another small bowl prepare Creamy Topping as directed. Remove slushy grape mixture from the freezer; beat just until smooth. Combine with beaten egg white and Creamy Topping in a bowl; beat on low speed until just blended. Spoon into a 5-cup dessert mold or freezer container. Cover and freeze. To serve, allow to soften 30 minutes in the refrigerator before turning out onto serving dish.

Yields 5 cups.

•Variations

Substitute your favorite fruit juice combinations.

JIFFY BANANA ICE CREAM

A quick and easy ice cream that's nutritious and delicious.

ICE CREAM: ¼ cup heavy cream or milk, ap-
4 ripe bananas, peeled and frozen   proximately

Slice frozen bananas. Whip in a food processor, gradually adding heavy cream or milk. Add just enough liquid until thick and
creamy. Spoon into sherbet dishes or over dessert and serve immediately.

                                                 Yields 1 to 2 cups.

ORANGE-PINEAPPLE CREAM

This large, impressive ice cream mold combines sweet cream and
fruit juice concentrate. Simple to make—and low-calorie, too!

MOLD: 1 6-oz. can unsweetened frozen
1 13-oz. can evaporated milk,   orange-pineapple juice con-
   well chilled   centrate, thawed

Chill bowl and beaters. Whip chilled evaporated milk in a large
bowl until stiff. (See Evaporated Milk, page 129, for more information.) Gradually beat in orange-pineapple juice concentrate. Spoon
mixture into a large 8-cup dessert mold or freezer containers. Store
frozen. To serve, invert mold onto serving dish. (There is no need
to thaw in refrigerator, as mold freezes to a soft consistency.) Garnish as desired.

                                                   Yields 8 cups.

●Variations

Apple Cream: Prepare as directed above, substituting unsweetened
frozen apple juice concentrate.

Pineapple Cream: Prepare as directed above, substituting unsweetened frozen pineapple juice concentrate.

Orange Cream: Prepare as directed above, substituting unsweetened frozen orange juice concentrate.

PINEAPPLE PARTY POPS

Sweet fruit juice concentrate and tangy buttermilk combine to make refreshing ice cream pops.

POPS:
1 tablespoon unflavored gelatin
   (1 packet)
¼ cup cold water

1 cup unsweetened frozen pineapple juice concentrate, thawed
1½ cups buttermilk
2 teaspoons vanilla extract

Sprinkle gelatin over cold water in a small bowl and allow to soften 5 minutes. Meanwhile, bring pineapple juice concentrate to a boil in a saucepan. Boil 3 minutes. (Frozen and fresh pineapple juice must be boiled 3 minutes to destroy an enzyme that interferes with proper gelatin.) Stir in softened gelatin, remove from heat, and cool to room temperature. Stir in buttermilk and vanilla extract. Pour mixture into a bowl and freeze, stirring occasionally, until mixture gels and thickens to the consistency of mashed potatoes. Remove from the freezer, beat, and pour into popsicle molds or 6-ounce paper cups. Insert sticks when partially frozen. Freeze.

To serve, dip popsicle molds briefly in warm water to loosen, or tear off paper cups. Serve immediately.

Yields 4 pops.

•Variations

Orange Party Pops: Prepare as directed above, substituting unsweetened frozen orange juice concentrate. (No need to boil 3 minutes.)

Pineapple-Orange Party Pops: Prepare as directed above, substituting unsweetened frozen pineapple-orange juice concentrate. (Boil 3 minutes.)

Apple Party Pops: Prepare as directed above, substituting unsweetened frozen apple juice concentrate. (No need to boil 3 minutes.)

ORANGE MINICREAMS

Tasty ice cream cupcakes.

CREAMS:
1 tablespoon unflavored gelatin
  (1 packet)
1 cup unsweetened frozen orange
  juice concentrate, thawed

1 cup buttermilk
Creamy Topping (see page 104)
2 teaspoons vanilla extract

Sprinkle gelatin over ½ cup thawed orange juice concentrate in a small bowl and allow to set 5 minutes to soften. Meanwhile, heat remaining ½ cup orange juice concentrate to a boil; stir in softened gelatin. Remove from the heat. Stir in buttermilk. Cool. Pour mixture into a 9" square pan, and freeze until firm but not frozen solid. Stir occasionally so that mixture freezes evenly.

Prepare Creamy Topping as directed; set aside. In a medium-sized bowl beat orange mixture and vanilla extract just until smooth. Fold in Creamy Topping. Spoon mixture into 12 foil-laminated medium-sized (2½") paper cupcake liners. Place filled liners on a cookie sheet and freeze. When frozen, desserts may be sealed in large plastic bags until ready to serve. Allow desserts to soften at room temperature 15 minutes before serving. Garnish as desired.

Yields 12 cupcakes.

•Variations

Apple Minicreams: Prepare as directed above, substituting unsweetened frozen apple juice concentrate.

Pineapple Minicreams: Prepare as directed above substituting unsweetened frozen pineapple juice concentrate; boil concentrate 3 minutes before using in the recipe, as it contains an enzyme that will otherwise interfere with proper gelation.

Gelatin Desserts

APRICOT REFRIGERATOR CAKE

A large, attractive gelatin cake with bright orange apricot layers and creamy frosting. Perfect for a summer buffet.

FILLING:
2 cups dried apricots
2 cups unsweetened pineapple juice
2 cups unsweetened orange juice
1 tablespoon vanilla extract
4 tablespoons unflavored gelatin (4 packets)
1 cup unsweetened orange juice, well chilled

FROSTING:
2 tablespoons unflavored gelatin (2 packets)
½ cup cold water
Double recipe of Creamy Topping (see page 104)

TOPPING:
1 small (8 oz.) can apricot halves in unsweetened juice

GARNISH:
Mint leaves
Cream Rosettes (see page 106)

Combine dried apricots and pineapple juice in a small saucepan. Bring to a boil, and cook covered over low heat for 20 minutes. Cool. Pour 2 cups of orange juice and 1 tablespoon vanilla extract in a blender. Gradually add apricot mixture and blend until smooth.

Sprinkle 4 tablespoons of gelatin over 1 cup of chilled orange juice and allow to set 5 minutes to soften. Place bowl containing softened gelatin over another filled with hot water (like a double boiler) and allow to dissolve into a clear liquid. If hot water cools before gelatin has dissolved, discard and replace with more hot water. If you prefer, gelatin may be dissolved in a small saucepan over low heat. Pour dissolved gelatin into blender and whip until blended. Refrigerate in a bowl until mixture reaches the consistency of mashed potatoes.

Next, prepare frosting. Sprinkle 2 tablespoons gelatin over ½ cup cold water and allow to soften and dissolve into a clear liquid, as directed previously. Cool to room temperature. Meanwhile, prepare Creamy Topping. Add dissolved gelatin and beat just to blend.

To assemble cake, spread half the apricot mixture evenly in a 9″ springform pan. Top with half the cream frosting, a second layer of apricot mixture, and, finally, top with the remaining cream frosting. If necessary, chill cake a short while to firm up a layer before topping with another. Refrigerate cake until firm.

To serve, drain can of apricot halves. Arrange apricot halves, rounded side up, in a ring on top of cake. Use a long sharp knife to loosen cake from pan sides. Remove pan sides. Slide cake, bottom metal plate attached, onto serving dish. Garnish plate or cake with mint leaves for added color, if desired. Cake also may be topped with Cream Rosettes.

Serves 10 to 12.

BLUEBERRY BAVARIAN

A sweet, light orange gelatin dessert filled with plump blueberries
and cream.

BAVARIAN:
2 tablespoons unflavored gelatin
  (2 packets)
½ cup cold water
1½ cups unsweetened orange
  juice

¼ teaspoon orange extract
1 teaspoon lemon juice
½ recipe Creamy Topping (see
  page 104)
2 cups fresh blueberries

Sprinkle unflavored gelatin over cold water in a small bowl and
allow to set 5 minutes to soften. Place bowl containing softened
gelatin over another filled with hot water (like a double boiler), and
set aside until gelatin dissolves into a clear liquid. If hot water cools
before gelatin has dissolved, discard and replace with more hot
water. If you prefer, gelatin may be dissolved in a small saucepan
over low heat. Meanwhile, combine orange juice, orange extract, and
lemon juice in a bowl. Stir in dissolved gelatin. Refrigerate until
mixture reaches a consistency slightly thicker than unbeaten egg
white.

Prepare Creamy Topping as directed. Fold Creamy Topping and
blueberries into partially gelled orange mixture. Spoon into a 4-cup
mold and refrigerate until mixture is firm. To serve, unmold onto
serving dish. May be garnished as desired with colorful fruit.

Serves 4.

PINEAPPLE SURPRISE

An impressive gelatin dessert with an outer layer of vanilla cream
and a surprise center of sweet pineapple and sliced banana.

FILLING:
2 tablespoons unflavored gelatin
   (2 packets)
½ cup cold water
3 cups unsweetened pineapple
   juice
1¾ cups sliced banana

FROSTING:
1 tablespoon unflavored gelatin
   (1 packet)
¼ cup cold water
Creamy Topping (see page 104)
1 teaspoon vanilla extract

Sprinkle 2 tablespoons gelatin over ½ cup cold water in a small
bowl and allow to soften 3 minutes. Bring pineapple juice to a boil.
(If using fresh or frozen pineapple juice, boil at least 3 minutes to
destroy an enzyme that interferes with proper gelation.) Stir in
softened gelatin. Cool and refrigerate until mixture reaches a consistency slightly thicker than unbeaten egg whites.

Meanwhile, prepare frosting. Soften 1 tablespoon gelatin over ¼
cup cold water in a small bowl. Place bowl containing softened
gelatin over another filled with hot water (like a double boiler), and
set aside while gelatin dissolves into a clear liquid. If hot water cools
before gelatin has dissolved, discard and replace with more hot
water. If you prefer, gelatin may be dissolved in a small saucepan
over low heat. Cool slightly to room temperature. Prepare Creamy
Topping as directed. Beat in vanilla extract and dissolved gelatin.
Spoon mixture into a 6-cup mold and chill 5 minutes or just until
it begins to gel. Remove from the refrigerator and spread cream
mixture evenly in the mold, covering the bottom and sides. Refrigerate.

When pineapple mixture is partially gelled, stir in sliced bananas
and spoon mixture into cream-lined mold. Chill until firm. To serve,
unmold onto serving dish and slice into pie-shaped wedges.

Serves 6.

COFFEE AND CREAM

This attractive two-tone gelatin dessert, filled with rich coffee flavor and orange sweetness, is a coffee-lovers' favorite.

MOLD:
2 tablespoons unflavored gelatin
 (two packets)
½ cup cold water
½ cup unsweetened frozen orange juice concentrate, thawed

1½ cups milk
2 teaspoons instant coffee
2 teaspoons vanilla extract
½ recipe Creamy Topping (see page 104)

Sprinkle gelatin over cold water in a small bowl. Allow to set 5 minutes to soften. Place bowl containing softened gelatin over another filled with hot water (like a double boiler), and set aside to dissolve into a clear liquid. If hot water cools before gelatin has dissolved, discard and replace with more hot water. If you prefer, gelatin may be dissolved in a small saucepan over low heat. Meanwhile, combine orange juice, milk, instant coffee, and vanilla extract in a blender (or bowl) and whip until smooth. Add dissolved gelatin and blend well.

Pour mixture into a bowl and refrigerate just a few minutes. Quickly, prepare Creamy Topping as directed. Reserve 1 cup of coffee mixture and fold Creamy Topping into the remainder. Spoon cream and coffee mixture into a 4-cup mold. Top with remaining coffee mixture. Refrigerate until firm.

Serves 4.

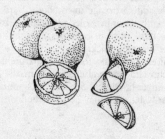

ORANGE-PINEAPPLE CHARLOTTE

A sensationally sweet filling surrounded by a ring of lady fingers, and generously garnished with fruit and whipped cream.

CAKE:
Approximately 30 lady fingers (see page 9)

FILLING:
2 tablespoons unflavored gelatin (2 packets)
½ cup cold water
1 6-oz. can unsweetened frozen pineapple juice concentrate, thawed
2 8-oz. packages cream cheese, softened

1 6-oz. can unsweetened frozen orange juice concentrate, thawed
1 tablespoon vanilla extract
3 egg whites, room temperature
¾ cup chopped walnuts (optional)

TOPPING:
Creamy Topping (see page 104)
Assorted fruit, fresh or canned

Make lady fingers as directed. Wet the inside edge of a 9" springform pan lightly with water. Line with lady fingers, pointed edges up, until pan edges are completely covered. Set aside.

To prepare filling, sprinkle gelatin over cold water in a small bowl. Allow to set 5 minutes to soften. Meanwhile, bring pineapple juice concentrate to a boil for 3 minutes, which is necessary for proper gelation. Stir in softened gelatin, remove from heat, and cool to room temperature. Beat cream cheese in a medium-sized bowl until creamy, gradually adding orange juice concentrate and vanilla extract. Beat thoroughly. Pour in cooled pineapple-gelatin mixture and beat. Refrigerate until mixture becomes firm, but not set. Check often, as mixture may gel quickly.

Whip egg whites until peaks form and mixture is firm. Fold egg whites and ½ cup chopped walnuts into partially gelled mixture. Spoon into lady-finger-lined pan. Sprinkle with remaining nuts. Refrigerate until set. Charlotte may be garnished with Creamy Topping and assorted fruits. To serve, run a sharp knife between lady fingers and pan edges. Remove sides, and slide charlotte, metal bottom attached, onto serving dish. Slice and serve as a cake.

Serves 8 to 10.

STRAWBERRY CREAM

A pineapple-cream center covered with colorful sliced strawberries.

MOLD:
3 tablespoons unflavored gelatin
 (3 packets)
¾ cup cold water
3 cups unsweetened pineapple
 juice

Creamy Topping (see page 104)

TOPPING:
2 cups sliced fresh strawberries

In a small bowl sprinkle gelatin over cold water, and allow to set 5 minutes to soften. Meanwhile, heat pineapple juice in a small saucepan. (If using fresh or frozen pineapple juice, boil 3 minutes to destroy an enzyme that interferes with proper gelation.) Stir softened gelatin into hot juice and allow it to dissolve. Cool to room temperature. Refrigerate, stirring mixture occasionally. When mixture reaches the consistency of unbeaten egg whites, line a 6-cup mold with sliced strawberries. Prepare Creamy Topping as directed and fold into pineapple mixture. Gently spoon into mold. Chill until firm.

To serve, invert onto serving plate. May be garnished with whole strawberries and whipped cream.

Serves 6.

CRANBERRY CHARLOTTE

An attractive charlotte filled with light apple-cranberry flavor and surrounded with delicate lady fingers.

FILLING:
3 tablespoons unflavored gelatin
  (3 packets)
¾ cup cold water
2½ cups unsweetened cranberry-
  apple juice
2 teaspoons lemon juice
Creamy Topping (see page 104)

CAKE:
Approximately 30 lady fingers
  (see page 9)

TOPPING:
1 fresh apple, peeled and thinly
  sliced
Creamy Frosting (see page 105)

Sprinkle gelatin over cold water in a small bowl. Allow to set 5 minutes to soften. Place bowl containing softened gelatin over another filled with hot water (like a double boiler) and set aside to dissolve into a clear liquid. If hot water cools before gelatin has dissolved, discard and replace with more hot water. If you prefer, gelatin may be dissolved in a small saucepan over low heat.

Combine cranberry-apple juice and lemon juice in a bowl. And dissolved gelatin and mix well. Refrigerate until mixture reaches a consistency slightly thicker than unbeaten egg whites. In a small bowl prepare Creamy Topping as directed. Fold into gelatin mixture.

Lightly wet the inside edge of a 9″ springform pan with water. Line with lady fingers, pointed edges up. Gently pour in filling and refrigerate to set. Shortly before serving, garnish top with Creamy Frosting and sliced apple. To serve, run a sharp knife between lady fingers and pan edge. Remove pan sides. Slide charlotte, metal bottom attached, onto serving dish. Slice and serve as a cake.

Serves 8 to 10.

EIGHT-LAYER STRAWBERRY CAKE

Sweet layers of sponge cake and pink strawberry-cream-cheese filling make this a most attractive dessert.

CAKE:
1 cup unbleached white flour
1/4 teaspoon baking soda
3/4 teaspoon baking powder
5 eggs, separated (room temperature)
1/2 cup unsweetened frozen pineapple juice concentrate, thawed
2 teaspoons vanilla extract

FILLING:
2 tablespoons unflavored gelatin (2 packets)

1/2 cup cold water
1/2 cup unsweetened pineapple-orange juice
1 20-oz. package frozen whole strawberries, thawed and sliced
1 8-oz. package cream cheese, softened
2 teaspoons vanilla extract

TOPPING:
Cream Rosettes (see page 106)
Whole strawberries, mint leaves (optional)

Line 2 9"-square baking pans with buttered wax paper. Set aside. Toss together flour, baking soda, and baking powder in a small bowl. Set aside. In a medium-sized mixing bowl beat together egg yolks, pineapple concentrate, and vanilla extract for 3 minutes or until fluffy and light. Fold in flour mixture and set aside.

In a separate bowl, and with clean beaters, beat egg whites until thick and peaks hold their shape. Gently fold pineapple mixture into egg whites. Divide batter evenly into wax paper-lined pans. Gently smooth batter in pans. Bake in a preheated oven at 325 degrees for 15 minutes or until firm. Cool 10 minutes in pans before turning out on wire racks to cool. Carefully peel off wax paper.

To make filling, sprinkle gelatin over cold water in a small bowl. Allow to set 5 minutes to soften. Bring pineapple-orange juice to a boil in a small saucepan. (Boil frozen or fresh juice 3 minutes to destroy an enzyme in pineapple that interferes with proper gelation.)

Stir softened gelatin into hot juice and remove from heat. Set aside to cool.

Drain juice from strawberries, which will yield about ¾ cup juice. Gradually add strawberry juice to cream cheese in a bowl and beat until smooth and creamy. Add vanilla extract and cooled pineapple juice. Beat until smooth. Refrigerate until thickened and partially set. Fold in strawberries.

To assemble, cut each cake in half horizontally and vertically, forming 8 4" by 4" squares. Completely open the pouring end of a half-gallon milk carton. Place alternate layers of cake and ½ cup filling in the carton. Press each cake square down into carton, using the blunt end of a knife, if necessary, to press corners into place. Occasionally dust knife end in flour to avoid sticking. End with layer of cake. Refrigerate several hours or overnight to set. To serve, carefully cut off paper carton that is laying on its side, and with a spatula place cake on a serving platter, still laying on its side. Garnish with Cream Rosettes, whole strawberries, and mint leaves, if desired. Cut into slices that include cake and filling. Cut each slice in half, serving two.

Serves 6 to 8.

GLORIOUS GRAPE GELATIN

Flavorful grape gelatin filled with sweet sliced banana.

GELATIN:
1½ tablespoons unflavored gelatin (1½ packets)

6 tablespoons cold water
3 cups unsweetened grape juice
4 cups sliced banana

In a small bowl sprinkle gelatin over cold water; set aside 5 minutes to soften. Meanwhile, bring grape juice to a boil and stir in softened gelatin. Cool to room temperature.

Refrigerate mixture, stirring occasionally, until it reaches a consistency slightly thicker than unbeaten egg whites. Stir in sliced banana. Spoon mixture into a 6-cup mold and chill until firm. To serve, unmold onto serving dish. Gelatin may be garnished as desired.

Serves 6.

PINEAPPLE GELATIN

A light but firm pineapple dessert full of sweet fruit.

GELATIN:
2 tablespoons unflavored gelatin
  (2 packets)
½ cup cold water
½ teaspoon lemon juice
¼ teaspoon cinnamon
¼ teaspoon orange extract (optional)

1 20-oz. can unsweetened crushed pineapple in natural juice

GARNISH:
Cream Rosettes (see page 106)

Sprinkle gelatin over cold water in a small bowl and allow to set 5 minutes to soften. Place bowl containing softened gelatin over a bowl filled with hot water (like a double boiler); set aside while gelatin dissolves into a clear liquid. If hot water cools before gelatin has dissolved, discard and replace with more hot water. If you prefer, gelatin may be dissolved in a small saucepan over low heat.

Meanwhile, mix the remaining ingredients in a blender until smooth. Add dissolved gelatin and whip until blended. Pour into a 3-cup mold and refrigerate until set. To serve, invert mold onto serving plate and garnish with Cream Rosettes as directed.

Serves 4.

STRAWBERRY GELATIN

A bright red gelatin full of naturally sweet strawberry flavor.

GELATIN:
2 tablespoons unflavored gelatin
   (2 packets)
½ cup cold water
1 12-oz. package frozen strawberries, loose pack and sugarfree,
   thawed

⅓ cup unsweetened frozen
   pineapple juice concentrate,
   thawed

GARNISH:
Creamy Topping (see page 104)
Strawberries

Sprinkle gelatin over cold water in a small bowl and allow to set 5 minutes to soften. Meanwhile, whip package of frozen strawberries, including juice, in a blender or food processor until smooth.

Bring pineapple juice concentrate to a boil in a small saucepan, boiling 3 minutes to destroy an enzyme that interferes with proper gelation. Stir in dissolved gelatin. Cool slightly. Pour into blender and whip thoroughly with strawberry purée. Pour mixture into 4 individual 6-ounce sherbet dishes. Chill until set. To serve, garnish with Creamy Topping and strawberries.

Serves 4.

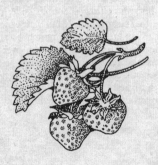

Pastries

CHOUX PASTRY (PUFF PASTRY)

A very light and soft pastry used for puff pastry desserts.

PASTRY:
1 cup water
½ cup butter

1 cup unbleached white flour
3 large eggs

In a medium-sized saucepan bring water and butter to a boil. Turn heat to low, add flour, and mix with a spoon until mixture becomes a cohesive ball. Remove pan from heat. Using an electric mixer, or mixing by hand, add 1 egg at a time and beat until thoroughly blended and smooth. Continue to add 1 egg at a time, beating well. Mixture will be shiny and smooth. Bake as directed in the following puff pastry recipes.

CHOCOLATE ECLAIRS

Rich pastry filled with vanilla cream and topped with a chocolate glaze.

PASTRY: TOPPING:
Choux Pastry (see page 59)   Chocolate Glaze (see page 110)

FILLING:
Vanilla Fluff (see page 107)

Make pastry as directed. Drop dough by tablespoons onto ungreased baking sheets. For each eclair, place 2 tablespoons dough with 2" in between. Spread to form 1" by 4" rectangles. Smooth the top and sides with a knife to mold uniformly shaped logs. Leave about 4" between each eclair. Bake in a preheated oven at 400 degrees for 25 to 30 minutes or until firm and well browned. Remove gently with a spatula to wire racks. Allow to cool.

Prepare filling and topping as directed. To assemble eclairs, slice tops off horizontally, and set tops aside. Scoop out any wet pastry and discard. Spoon Vanilla Fluff into eclairs, replace tops, and spread with Chocolate Icing. Store eclairs in a deep baking pan covered with plastic wrap or aluminum foil, and refrigerate.

Yields 12.

• Note: Fill eclairs shortly before serving so that the pastry remains crisp and light.

•Variations

Fruit Eclairs: Stir sliced fresh fruit into filling.

Cocoa Chocolate Eclairs: Prepare as directed above, and fill with Heavenly Cocoa Mousse (see page 24).

FLUFFY LEMON CREAM PUFFS

Light pastry desserts filled with a melt-in-your-mouth lemon filling and topped with a chocolate glaze.

PASTRY:
Choux Pastry (see page 59)

TOPPING:
Chocolate Glaze (see page 110)

FILLING:
Lemon Fluff (see page 108)

Make pastry as directed. Drop dough by tablespoons onto ungreased baking sheets, leaving 2″ between each spoonful. With a sharp knife gently shape each into a mound, pointing up in the center. Bake in a preheated oven at 400 degrees for 25 to 30 minutes or until browned and firm. Remove with a spatula and cool on wire racks.

Prepare Lemon Fluff and Chocolate Glaze as directed. To assemble cream puffs, slice the tops off each pastry. Scoop out and discard any wet dough. Fill each pastry with filling, replace tops, and top with Chocolate Glaze. Store cream puffs in a deep baking pan, cover, and refrigerate.

Yields 24.

• *Note:* Fill cream puffs shortly before serving so that the pastry remains crisp and light.

•Variations

Fruit Cream Puffs: Stir sliced fresh fruit into filling.

PEACH MERINGUE PASTRY RINGS

Light pastry rings filled with spicy peach meringue and sliced peaches.

PASTRY:
Choux Pastry (see page 59)

FILLING:
2 tablespoons unflavored gelatin (2 packets)
½ cup cold water
2 16-oz. cans sliced peaches in unsweetened juice, well drained (or 3 cups sliced fresh peaches)
1 teaspoon vanilla extract

½ teaspoon lemon juice
½ teaspoon cinnamon
2 tablespoons unsweetened frozen orange juice concentrate (do not use pineapple)
4 egg whites, room temperature
½ recipe Creamy Topping (see page 104)

TOPPING:
1½ cups sliced fresh peaches (or well-drained canned peaches)

Prepare pastry as directed. Place the rim of a 4″ cookie cutter into water and then into flour. Press repeatedly on an ungreased cookie sheet to outline 8 circles at least 2″ apart. Next, place the rim of a 2½″ cookie cutter (or jar cover) into water and then flour. Press onto cookie sheet to outline smaller circles centered within larger ones, forming rings. Using about 3 tablespoons of pastry per ring, follow outlines and spread dough with a knife to form rings with smooth tops and sides. Bake in a preheated oven at 400 degrees for 20 minutes or until browned and firm. Remove rings gently with a spatula and cool on wire racks.

To make filling, sprinkle gelatin over cold water in a small bowl and allow to soften 5 minutes. Place bowl containing softened gelatin over another filled with hot water (like a double boiler); set aside to dissolve into a clear liquid. If hot water cools before gelatin has dissolved, discard and replace with more hot water. If you prefer, gelatin may be dissolved in a small saucepan over low heat. Meanwhile, whip together sliced peaches, vanilla extract, lemon juice, cinnamon, and orange juice concentrate in a blender until smooth and creamy. Pour in dissolved gelatin and whip thoroughly. Pour into a bowl. Refrigerate until partially set, but not firm. When partially set, whip egg whites at high speed until thick and fluffy. Prepare Creamy Topping as directed. Fold both into peach mixture until well blended. Refrigerate until serving.

To serve, place a pastry ring on each dessert plate. Top generously with peach filling and garnish with sliced peaches. Serve immediately.

Serves 8.

MERINGUE SHELLS

Very light meringue dessert shells, golden brown and ready to fill with pudding, ice cream, whipped cream, or sliced fresh fruit.

SHELLS:
4 egg whites, room temperature
1/8 teaspoon salt
1/2 teaspoon cream of tartar
1/2 teaspoon vanilla extract

Beat egg whites until foamy. Add salt and cream of tartar. Continue beating until egg whites are firm. Do not underbeat. Add vanilla extract; beat briefly to blend. Divide egg whites into 6 equal mounds on a large greased cookie sheet. Using 2 tablespoons, gently shape mounds into 4½" circles. Indent a large hollow in the center of each, using the back of a spoon.

Bake meringues in a preheated oven at 275 degrees for 45 minutes or until firm to the touch and lightly browned. Cool on a wire rack. Meringues may be filled shortly before serving with any of the following: pudding, custard, ice cream, sherbet, whipped cream, chopped fruit, etc.

Serves 6.

COCOA NAPOLEON

An impressive Napoleon with paper-thin pastry and a cocoa cream filling, and garnished with rosettes.

PASTRY:
15 12" by 16" sheets of strudel pastry (available in supermarket frozen-food section)
¼ cup melted butter, approximately

FILLING:
Heavenly Cocoa Mousse (see page 24)

GARNISH:
Cream Rosettes (see page 106)

Thaw strudel pastry as directed on package. Brush each pastry sheet with melted butter, and fold in half to form a 6" by 16" rectangle. Place one on top of another on a large, ungreased baking sheet. Brush the top with butter. Bake in a preheated oven at 375 degrees for 10 to 15 minutes or until lightly browned around the edges. With a sharp knife cut ¼" from edges to shape pastry. Using 2 spatulas, lift pastry onto a wire rack to cool completely.

Prepare filling as directed and refrigerate until just firm enough to hold its shape. Gently pry pastry sheets apart into 3 equal sections Spread filling over each layer, and restack. Place dessert on a serving platter and decorate with rosettes. Colorful fruits may also be added as a garnish. To serve, slice into 2" portions.

Serves 8.

PASTRY SHORTCAKES

Light and rich little layer cakes filled with vanilla cream and topped with fruit.

PASTRY:
10 12" by 16" sheets of strudel pastry (available in supermarket frozen-food section)
¼ cup melted butter, approximately

FILLING:
Double recipe of Vanilla Fluff (see page 107)
Creamy Topping (see page 104)

GARNISH:
Fresh fruit or whole berries

Thaw pastry sheets as directed. To prepare pastry, lay one sheet of pastry on a flat surface and brush with melted butter. Cover with another pastry sheet, melted butter, and continue until all sheets are stacked. Brush top with butter.

Using a 4" round cookie cutter and sharp knife, cut through pastry stack to form 12 4" round circles. Lift each circle with a spatula onto an ungreased baking sheet. Bake in a preheated oven at 375 degrees for 10 to 12 minutes or until lightly browned. Watch closely, as they brown quickly. Cool on a wire rack.

Prepare Vanilla Fluff and Creamy Topping, and fold together. Separate each circle into 3 or 4 pastry layers. Restack pastry, covering each layer with filling. Top with a spoonful of filling. Cakes may be garnished with fresh fruit, whole berries, or Chocolate Icing (see page 110). Store refrigerated.

Serves 12.

BLUEBERRY CREAM PASTRY TORTE

This light torte is composed of light paper-thin pastry layers laced
with a creamy filling and blueberries.

PASTRY:
*8 12" by 16" sheets of strudel
pastry (available in supermarket frozen-food section)*
*¼ cup melted butter butter, ap-
proximately*

FILLING:
*Double recipe Creamy Topping
(see page 104)*
*1 pint fresh blueberries (approxi-
mately 3 cups)*

Thaw pastry as directed on the package. Lay a pastry sheet out
on a flat surface and brush with melted butter. Cover with another
sheet, brush with butter, and repeat until all sheets are stacked.
Brush top sheet with butter.

Invert a 9" or 10" cake pan over pastry stack and trace edges with
a sharp knife, cutting out a pastry circle. With spatulas, lift circle
onto a ungreased baking sheet. Bake in a preheated oven at 375
degrees for 8 minutes or until lightly browned. Cool on a wire rack.

Prepare Creamy Topping as directed; fold in blueberries. To
assemble pry pastry sheets apart into 4 thin layers. Place one pastry
layer on a serving dish, top evenly with filling, and repeat until all
layers are stacked and top sheet is covered with filling. Store refrigerated. To serve, cut into pie-shaped wedges.

Serves 6 to 8.

FRENCH PEAR GALETTE

A rich open-faced pie covered with overlapping rings of spicy pear slices.

PASTRY:
1½ cups unbleached white flour
½ cup chilled butter (or shortening)
4 tablespoons cold water, approximately

TOPPING:
4 cups thinly sliced fresh pear (4 to 5 pears)
1 teaspoon lemon juice
¼ teaspoon cinnamon
¼ teaspoon nutmeg
1 tablespoon butter

Mix together flour and butter (or shortening) until crumbly. Gradually add water, adding just enough to form a soft dough. Roll into a ball, flatten, wrap in plastic wrap, and refrigerate until firm. Roll pastry out on a lightly floured surface to approximately a 13″ diameter circle, ⅛″ thick. Roll pastry up on a rolling pin, and unroll onto a large ungreased baking sheet. Starting 1″ in from the edge, form a circle of overlapping pear slices. (Have long sides pointing toward pie center and overlap shorter sides.) Form a second row, overlapping it slightly over first row. Continue until pastry is completely covered with rings of sliced pears, forming a pattern similar to a rose.

Sprinkle lemon juice, spices, and bits of butter over pears. Fold the outside edge of the pastry up over pears, and press securely in place. Bake in a preheated oven at 400 degrees for 50 to 60 minutes or until nicely browned. Serve warm or cooled. Cut into pie-shaped wedges.

Serves 8 to 10.

•Variations

Apple Galette: Prepare as directed above, substituting sliced apples for pears.

Peach Galette: Prepare as directed above, substituting sliced peaches for pears.

Pies

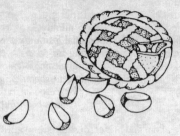

THANKSGIVING PIE

Creamy, flavorful, and delightfully spicy.

PASTRY:
1¼ cups unbleached white flour
3 tablespoons chilled butter (or shortening)
5 tablespoons cold water, approximately

FILLING:
3 large eggs
1½ cups cooked pumpkin (or squash)

½ cup mashed banana (mash ripe banana with a fork)
1 teaspoon vanilla extract
1 teaspoon cinnamon
1½ teaspoons nutmeg
⅛ teaspoon ginger
⅛ teaspoon cloves
1½ cups light cream or half-and-half

TOPPING:
Nutmeg

Mix together flour and butter (or shortening). Gradually add water, adding just enough to form a soft dough. Roll out on a floured surface to ⅛″ thickness. Place pastry sheet in a 9″ pie pan, trim off excess, and flute edges. Gather together excess pastry, mix, and roll out to ⅛″ thickness. Cut pastry with cookie cutters in attractive shapes. Place pastries on a small ungreased cookie sheet, and prick well with a fork. Set aside.

Using a blender or mixer, whip together all filling ingredients until smooth. Pour into pastry-lined pie pan. Sprinkle with nutmeg. Place both pie and baking sheet with pastries into a preheated 425 degree oven. Remove baking sheet after 5 minutes, and cool pastries on a wire rack. Allow the pie an additional 5 minutes, then reduce heat to 350 degrees, and continue baking for 40 more minutes or until pie has set (a knife inserted comes out clean). Remove pie from oven and top with pastry shapes, pressing gently into pie filling. Cool and store refrigerated.

Serves 6 to 8.

APPLE CUSTARD PIE

A spicy custard pie filled with sweet apple slices. Good nutrition never tasted so good!

PASTRY:
1 cup unbleached white flour
3 tablespoons chilled butter (or shortening)
4 tablespoons unsweetened apple juice, approximately

FILLING:
2 cups thinly sliced fresh apple (peel, core, and slice 2 medium-sized apples)

¼ teaspoon nutmeg
½ teaspoon cinnamon
1 tablespoon unbleached white flour
1 cup unsweetened applesauce
1 cup milk
2 teaspoons vanilla extract
3 large eggs
¼ cup unbleached white flour

Mix flour and butter (or shortening) until blended. Gradually add apple juice, adding just enough to form a soft dough. Roll pastry out on a floured surface to ⅛" thickness. Fit into a 9" pie pan, trim off excess pastry, and flute edges.

Toss together sliced apples with spices and 1 tablespoon flour.

Spread apple mixture evenly in pastry-lined pie pan. Using a blender
or mixer, whip together remaining filling ingredients until smooth.
Gently pour into pie pan over apple slices. Bake pie in a preheated
oven at 400 degrees for 10 minutes; reduce heat to 350 degrees, and
continue baking for an additional 50 to 60 minutes or until custard
has set. Cool on a wire rack and store refrigerated.

Serves 6 to 8.

•Variations

Peach Custard Pie: Prepare pie as directed above, substituting sliced
peaches for sliced apples.

Pear Custard Pie: Prepare pie as directed above, substituting sliced
pears for sliced apples.

COCOA BANANA CREAM PIE

A very light pie with filling that melts in your mouth. A favorite with
kids.

PASTRY:
1 cup unbleached white flour
1 tablespoon unsweetened cocoa
   (or carob powder)
¼ cup chilled butter (or shortening)
3 tablespoons cold water, approximately

FILLING:
1 tablespoon unflavored gelatin
   (1 package)

¼ cup cold water
2 cups mashed banana (mash
   ripe banana with a fork)
1 teaspoon lemon juice
2 teaspoons vanilla extract
1 tablespoon unsweetened cocoa
   (or carob powder)
Creamy Topping (see page 104)

TOPPING:
Cream Rosettes (see page 106)

Mix together flour, cocoa, and butter (or shortening) until blended. Gradually add water, adding just enough to form a soft dough. Roll pastry out on a floured surface to ⅛″ thickness, and fit into a 9″ pie pan. Trim off excess pastry and flute edges. Prick with a fork. Bake in a preheated oven at 425 degrees for 8 to 10 minutes. Remove to a wire rack and cool. Store refrigerated.

To prepare filling, sprinkle gelatin over cold water in a small bowl and allow to set 5 minutes to soften. Then place the bowl of softened gelatin over another filled with hot water (like a double boiler), and set aside while gelatin dissolves into a clear liquid. If hot water cools before gelatin has dissolved, discard and replace with more hot water. If you prefer, gelatin may be dissolved in a small saucepan over low heat.

Meanwhile, beat together mashed banana, lemon juice, vanilla extract, and cocoa at high speed 2 or 3 minutes. Mixture will be smooth and fluffy. Add dissolved gelatin and beat until blended. Refrigerate mixture until slightly thicker than unbeaten egg whites. In a small bowl prepare Creamy Topping as directed; fold into cocoa mixture. Spoon into pastry-lined pie pan. Prepare Cream Rosettes as directed, completely covering the pie top. Refrigerate until serving.

Serves 6 to 8.

PEACHY YOGURT PIE

A quick, nutritious, no-bake pie you can whip up in the blender. Full of spicy peach flavor.

CRUST:
2 tablespoons melted butter
1 cup flaked coconut

FILLING:
2 tablespoons unflavored gelatin
(2 packets)
½ cup cold water
1 29-oz. can sliced peaches in unsweetened juice, well drained

1 cup plain yogurt
1 tablespoon vanilla extract
¼ teaspoon orange extract
½ teaspoon cinnamon

TOPPING:
2 tablespoons flaked coconut
1 small (8 oz.) can sliced peaches
in unsweetened juice, well
drained

To prepare crust toss together melted butter and flaked coconut in a 9" pie pan. Sprinkle evenly over pie pan bottom and sides. Refrigerate.

In a small bowl sprinkle gelatin over cold water, and allow to set 5 minutes to soften. Place bowl containing softened gelatin over another filled with hot water (like a double boiler) and set aside while gelatin dissolves into a clear liquid. If hot water cools before gelatin has dissolved, discard and replace with more hot water. If you prefer, gelatin may be dissolved in a small saucepan over low heat. Meanwhile, drain 29-ounce can of sliced peaches and whip peaches in a blender until smooth. Add remaining filling ingredients and whip. Add dissolved gelatin and blend well. Pour mixture into coconut-lined pie pan and refrigerate. When pie filling is firm, drain small can of sliced peaches and arrange peach slices over pie. Sprinkle with flaked coconut. Store refrigerated.

Serves 6 to 8.

SOUR CREAM RAISIN PIE

A sweet, creamy pie filled with plump raisins.

PASTRY:
1 cup unbleached white flour
3 tablespoons chilled butter (or shortening)
4 tablespoons cold water, approximately

FILLING:
1 large egg
2 cups milk
½ cup cornstarch
2 cups sour cream
½ teaspoon cinnamon
½ teaspoon nutmeg
1 tablespoon vanilla extract
1½ cups raisins

To prepare pastry, mix together flour and butter (or shortening) until evenly blended. Gradually add water, adding just enough to form a soft dough. Roll pastry out on a lightly floured surface to ⅛" thickness. Fit pastry sheet into a 9" pie pan, trim off excess pastry, and flute edges. Bake in a preheated oven at 425 degrees for 8 to 10 minutes, or until lightly browned. Cool on a wire rack.

In the top of a double boiler mix together egg, milk, and cornstarch. Cook over simmering water, stirring constantly, for 10 minutes. Mixture will be smooth and thick. Remove from the heat and allow to cool to room temperature. Beat in sour cream, spices, and vanilla extract until smooth. Stir in raisins. Spoon mixture into the prebaked pie shell. Refrigerate until firm.

Serves 6 to 8.

•Variation

Yogurt Raisin Pie: Prepare as directed above substituting plain yogurt for sour cream.

GRETTLE'S CAKE AND PIE

An unusual pie consisting of a thick bottom layer of spicy cake and a generous topping of apple and raisin glaze.

CAKE:
¼ cup butter, softened (or shortening)
1 large egg
1 teaspoon vanilla extract
½ cup unsweetened frozen apple
   juice concentrate, thawed
1 cup unbleached white flour
¼ teaspoon baking powder
¼ teaspoon baking soda

¼ teaspoon cinnamon
¼ teaspoon nutmeg

TOPPING:
3 cups thinly sliced apple (peel,
   core, and slice 3 or 4 apples)
1 cup unsweetened apple juice
½ cup raisins
2 tablespoons cornstarch
¼ cup cold water

Beat together butter (or shortening) and egg until creamy. Add vanilla extract, juice concentrate, and beat well. Measure in remaining dry ingredients. Beat just until smooth. Spoon batter into an oiled and floured 9" pie pan. Bake in a preheated oven at 325 degrees for 20 to 25 minutes or until firm. Cool on a wire rack. Do not remove cake from the pan.

To prepare topping, combine sliced apples, apple juice, and raisins in a small saucepan. Bring to a boil, turn to low, and simmer covered 5 minutes to soften apples. Remove from the heat. Strain apples and catch the juice in a bowl. Return the juice to saucepan. Combine cornstarch and cold water; mix well. Add to apple juice. Bring to a boil, stirring constantly, and boil 1 minute. Remove from heat. Stir into sliced apples, and cool mixture to room temperature.

Spoon apple mixture over cake, still in pan. Refrigerate to set. To serve, cut into pie-shaped wedges.

Serves 6 to 8.

APPLE FRUIT PIE

A sweet, juicy, apple-raisin-and-date-filled pie, topped with an attractive lattice pastry crust.

FILLING:
½ cup raisins
½ cup chopped dates, pits removed
¾ cup water
4 cups thinly sliced apple (peel, core, and slice 5 or 6 apples)
1 teaspoon lemon juice
1 teaspoon cinnamon
½ teaspoon nutmeg
¼ cup unbleached white flour

PASTRY:
2 cups unbleached white flour
⅔ cup chilled butter (or shortening)
4 tablespoons unsweetened apple juice, approximately

Combine raisins, dates, and water in a small saucepan. Cover and bring to a boil. Turn to low and simmer 10 minutes. Remove from the heat and cool. Whip in a blender until smooth. Meanwhile, toss together sliced apples and remaining filling ingredients. Add date-raisin mixture and mix well. Refrigerate.

To prepare pastry, combine flour and butter (or shortening) until evenly blended. Gradually add apple juice, adding just enough to form a soft dough. Roll ⅔ out on a lightly floured surface to ⅛" thickness. Fit into a 9" pie pan, trimming off excess pastry. Gather together all remaining pastry, roll as previously, and cut into ½" wide lattice strips.

Spoon filling into pie shell and top with lattice strips, placing strips close together so pie filling will not dry out during baking. Flute edges. Bake in a preheated oven at 450 degrees for 10 minutes; reduce temperature to 350 degrees and continue baking 40 minutes more or until apples are tender. Cool on a wire rack. Serve warm or chilled.

Serves 8 to 10.

•Variation

Pear Fruit Pie: Prepare as directed above, substituting sliced pears for sliced apples.

RHUBARB-PINEAPPLE PIE

Frozen rhubarb and canned pineapple combine to make a sweet and delicious fruit pie.

PASTRY:
2 cups unbleached white flour
⅔ cup chilled butter (or shortening)
4 tablespoons unsweetened pineapple juice, approximately

FILLING:
1 10-oz. package frozen rhubarb, thawed and drained (or 2 cups fresh rhubarb, cut in ½" slices)
2 20-oz. cans crushed pineapple in unsweetened juice
½ cup unbleached white flour
¼ teaspoon cinnamon
2 teaspoons lemon juice

To prepare pastry, mix together flour and butter (or shortening) until crumbly. Gradually add pineapple juice, adding just enough to form a soft dough. Roll ⅔ of the dough out on a lightly floured surface to ⅛" thickness. Fit into a 9" pie pan, and trim off excess pastry. Roll out remaining dough and set aside.

Combine all filling ingredients in a bowl and mix well. Spoon into pastry-lined pie pan. Top with pastry sheet and flute edges securely together. Slit pastry to allow steam to escape during baking. Bake in a preheated oven at 375 degrees for 40 minutes or until rhubarb is tender and pastry is lightly browned. Cool and store refrigerated.

Serves 6 to 8.

Quiches and Kuchens

BLUEBERRY QUICHE

A colorful quiche filled with generous layers of blueberries and cheesy filling, and topped with swirls of blueberry syrup.

PASTRY:
1 cup unbleached white flour
3 tablespoons chilled butter (or shortening)
4 tablespoons cold water, approximately

1 8-oz. package cream cheese, softened
4 egg yolks
1 cup heavy cream
2 teaspoons unbleached white flour

FILLING:
1 12-oz. package frozen whole blueberries, loose pack and sugarfree, thawed

TOPPING:
1 teaspoon unsweetened frozen pineapple juice concentrate
1 teaspoon cornstarch

Mix together flour and butter (or shortening). Gradually add water, adding just enough to form a soft dough. Roll out on a floured surface to ⅛" thickness. Place in a 9" pie pan, trim off excess pastry, and flute edges.

To prepare filling, drain thawed blueberries, catching juice in a small saucepan. Set aside. Beat together cream cheese and egg yolks until smooth and creamy. Gradually add heavy cream, beating just until light and fluffy. Sprinkle 2 teaspoons of flour over unbaked pie shell. Cover evenly with drained blueberries, reserving juice for topping. Gently spoon in cheese filling, being careful not to disturb berries. Bake in a preheated oven at 375 degrees for 45 to 50 minutes. Quiche will be nicely browned. Cool on a wire rack.

To make topping, combine juice drained from blueberries (½ to ⅓ cup), pineapple concentrate, and cornstarch in a small saucepan. Mix well. Cook over medium heat, stirring constantly, until mixture reaches a boil. Remove from heat and drop by spoonfulls in a spiral pattern over quiche. Refrigerate and serve well chilled.

Serves 6 to 8.

TRIPLE DATE QUICHE

A very sweet quiche filled with grated cheese, chopped dried dates, and rich milk custard.

PASTRY:
1 cup unbleached white flour
1 tablespoon cream cheese
2 tablespoons chilled butter (or shortening)
3 tablespoons (approximately) unsweetened apple juice, chilled

FILLING:
3 tablespoons grated cheese (cheddar, Romano, or Parmesan)

1½ cups finely chopped dates, pits removed
1 tablespoon unbleached white flour
3 large eggs
3 tablespoons unbleached white flour
1 cup milk
½ teaspoon vanilla extract

TOPPING:
Nutmeg

Mix together flour, cream cheese, and butter (or shortening) until evenly blended. Gradually add apple juice, adding just enough to form a soft dough. Refrigerate dough until firm. Roll out on a lightly floured surface to ⅛" thickness. Place in a 9" pie pan, trim off excess pastry, and flute edges.

To prepare filling, sprinkle grated cheese evenly over pie crust bottom. Toss chopped dates with 1 tablespoon flour, and pour into pie crust, covering bottom evenly. In a small mixing bowl, beat together eggs and 3 tablespoons flour until blended. Add milk and vanilla extract. Beat just until mixed. Pour slowly into pie crust, covering dates. Gently press down any dates that rise above custard level. Sprinkle with nutmeg. Bake in a preheated oven at 350 degrees for 40 minutes or until custard has set. Cool and refrigerate.

Serves 6 to 8.

PEACH CUSTARD QUICHE

A flavorful and nutritious custard quiche filled with sweet and spicy peaches.

PASTRY:
1 cup unbleached white flour
3 tablespoons chilled butter (or shortening)
4 tablespoons cold water, approximately

½ teaspoon cinnamon
2 tablespoons unbleached white flour
4 large eggs
1¼ cups heavy cream
2 teaspoons vanilla extract

FILLING:
1 16-oz. can sliced peaches in unsweetened juice (or 1½ cups sliced fresh peaches)

TOPPING:
Nutmeg

To prepare pastry, mix together flour and butter (or shortening) until evenly mixed. Gradually add water, adding just enough to form a soft dough. Roll out on a lightly floured surface to ⅛" thickness. Place in a 9" pie pan, trim off excess pastry, and flute edges.

Drain canned peaches. Toss peaches with cinnamon and 2 tablespoons flour. Place in a spiral pattern in the bottom of the pastry-lined pie pan. In a medium-sized mixing bowl, beat eggs until fluffy. Add cream and vanilla extract. Beat until blended. Pour over sliced peaches. Sprinkle pie generously with nutmeg. Bake in a preheated oven at 350 degrees for 60 minutes or until nicely browned and filling has set. Cool on a wire rack and store refrigerated.

Serves 6 to 8.

APRICOT KUCHEN

A delicious and attractive kuchen with a filling of sweet white cream and topping of colorful orange apricots.

PASTRY:
1¼ cups unbleached white flour
½ cup chilled butter (or shortening)
3 tablespoons yogurt (or sour cream)
1 teaspoon cinnamon

FILLING:
⅓ cup heavy cream

2 egg yolks
¼ cup unbleached white flour
1 teaspoon vanilla extract

TOPPING:
1 16-oz. can apricot halves in unsweetened juice (or 7 whole fresh apricots, peeled, halved, and pits removed)

To prepare pastry, mix together flour and butter (or shortening) until blended. Add remaining pastry ingredients and mix. Dipping your fingers occasionally in flour, press pastry mixture evenly in a 9" tart pan, covering bottom and sides. (If you don't have a tart pan, use a 9" pie pan.) Bake in a preheated oven at 375 degrees for 15 minutes.

Meanwhile, combine all the filling ingredients and beat well. When pastry is done, remove from the oven, and pour in cream filling. Top with well-drained canned apricots (or fresh apricot halves), rounded sides up. Continue baking for 20 to 25 minutes more or until filling is lightly browned. Cool and refrigerate. To serve, remove tart from pan, and place on serving dish.

Serves 6 to 8.

•Variations

You may substitute your choice of well-drained canned fruit or sliced fresh fruit for topping and bake as directed.

PEACHES AND CREAM KUCHEN

A sweet cake layer covered with sour cream and topped with sliced peaches.

PASTRY:
1 large egg
1 cup unsweetened frozen orange juice concentrate, thawed
⅓ cup melted butter
1½ cups unbleached white flour
¼ teaspoon baking powder
¼ teaspoon baking soda

FILLING:
1 cup sour cream (or plain yogurt)

⅓ cup unbleached white flour
1 teaspoon vanilla extract
¼ teaspoon cinnamon
1 tablespoon unsweetened frozen orange juice concentrate, thawed

TOPPING:
1 16-oz. can sliced peaches in unsweetened juice (or 1½ cups sliced fresh peaches)

Beat together egg, orange juice concentrate, and butter. Add remaining pastry ingredients and mix until evenly blended. Press evenly in the bottom of an oiled and floured 8″ or 9″ springform pan. Bake in a preheated oven at 350 degrees for 15 minutes.

Meanwhile, combine filling ingredients and beat just until blended. When pastry is done, remove from the oven, and spread evenly with filling ingredients. Arrange a ring of well-drained canned peaches (or fresh peach slices) over filling. Return to the oven and

continue baking for 15 more minutes. Cool on a wire rack and
refrigerate. To serve, remove sides of springform pan. Slide kuchen
off metal pan bottom and onto serving dish. Cut into pie-shaped
wedges.

Serves 6 to 8.

Tarts

APPLE RAISIN TART

A large tart filled with apples, raisins, and cranberries, and covered with a sweet whipped-cream lattice topping.

PASTRY:
1 egg yolk
6 tablespoons chilled butter (or shortening)
1 tablespoon lemon juice
1 tablespoon frozen unsweetened apple juice concentrate, thawed
1 cup unbleached white flour, approximately

FILLING:
½ cup raisins
½ cup unsweetened apple juice
3 cups thinly sliced apple (peel, core, and slice approximately 4 apples)

1 teaspoon lemon juice
¼ cup thinly sliced fresh cranberries
3 tablespoons unbleached white flour
½ teaspoon cinnamon
½ teaspoon nutmeg
1 tablespoon unbleached white flour

TOPPING:
Lattice Cream Topping (see page 108)

Cream together egg yolk and butter (or shortening). Add lemon juice and apple concentrate. Gradually add flour, adding just enough to form a soft dough. Roll into a ball, flatten, wrap in plastic wrap, and refrigerate until firm. When firm, roll out pastry on a floured surface. Fit into an 8" tart pan or 8" pie pan. Press pastry evenly in pan, covering the bottom and 1" up the sides. Refrigerate.

To prepare filling, combine raisins and apple juice in a small saucepan. Cover, bring to a boil, remove from heat, and let stand covered 10 minutes to soften. Meanwhile, toss sliced apples with lemon juice. Add cranberries, 3 tablespoons flour, and spices; toss well. Add raisin mixture, including juice, and mix.

Sprinkle 1 tablespoon of flour over pastry bottom. Spoon in fruit filling, mounding it up in the center. Cut a circle of aluminum foil and lay over filling, leaving side pastry edges exposed. Bake in a preheated oven at 400 degrees for 30 minutes. Remove from the oven, and place on a wire rack to cool. Remove foil cover. Before serving remove tart from tart pan, and decorate with Lattice Cream Topping as directed.

Serves 6.

PINEAPPLE TARTS

Sweet pineapple filling in individual tart pastries.

PASTRY:
1¼ cups unbleached white flour
¼ cup chilled butter (or shortening)
¼ teaspoon cinnamon
¼ teaspoon almond extract

4 tablespoons chilled unsweetened pineapple juice, approximately

FILLING:
Pineapple Topping (see page 112)

To prepare pastry, mix together flour, butter (or shortening), cinnamon, and almond extract. Gradually add pineapple juice, adding just enough to form a soft dough. Pinch off pieces of dough, and press evenly in individual tart pans, covering the bottom and sides with a thin layer of pastry dough. (If tart pans are not available, you may use small-sized muffin pans.)

Place pastry-lined tart pans on a baking sheet, prick with a fork, and freeze until firm. Bake in a preheated oven at 475 degrees for 5 minutes or until lightly browned. Baking time will vary slightly depending on the size of tart pans and thickness of dough, so check to avoid overbaking. Cool pastry 10 minutes in the pans on wire racks. Remove tart pans by inverting over wire racks and tapping pans lightly. Turn pastry right side up and cool.

Prepare Pineapple Topping as directed. When partially gelled, spoon into individual tart pastries. Refrigerate until serving. May be garnished as desired.

Yields 18 to 20 2" tarts.

•Variations

Blackberry Tarts: Prepare Ritz Blackberry Pudding (see page 26). When cooled to room temperature, spoon into tart pastries and refrigerate. Attractive when decorated with whipped cream.

Raspberry Tarts: Prepare Ritz Raspberry Pudding (see page 25). When cooled to room temperature, spoon into tart pastries and refrigerate.

STRAWBERRY TARTS

Little tart pastries filled with red strawberry gelatin.

PASTRY: FILLING:
*Pineapple Tart pastry (see page   Strawberry Gelatin (see page 58)
84)*

Make pastry as directed and bake; set aside. Prepare Strawberry Gelatin. When gelatin reaches a consistency slightly thicker than unbeaten egg white, spoon into tart shells. Refrigerate to set and garnish as desired.

Yields 18 to 20 2" tarts.

●Variation

Strawberry Pudding Tarts: Prepare Strawberry Pudding as directed (see page 26). When cooled to room temperature, spoon into tart pastry and refrigerate.

LATTICE PEAR TART

A large, impressive tart filled with spicy pear and topped with attractive lattice pastry.

PASTRY:
2¼ cups unbleached white flour
1 cup chilled butter (see note below)
¼ teaspoon almond extract
1 teaspoon cinnamon
3 tablespoons cold water, approximately

FILLING:
5 cups chopped fresh pear (peel, core, and chop pears)
1 teaspoon lemon juice
⅓ cup unbleached white flour
1 teaspoon nutmeg
¾ teaspoon cinnamon
⅓ cup heavy cream

To prepare pastry, mix together flour, butter, almond extract, and cinnamon. Gradually add water, adding just enough to form a soft dough. Roll ⅔ of the pastry into a ball, flatten, wrap in plastic wrap, and refrigerate. Do the same with the remaining dough. Store refrigerated until firm. When firm, roll out larger piece of pastry on a floured surface to ⅛" thickness. Fit into an 11" tart pan. (If you do not have a large tart pan, use a large pie pan.) Press pastry into pan and trim off excess. Refrigerate while preparing filling.

Toss chopped pears with lemon juice, flour, and spices. Spread evenly in pastry-lined tart pan. Drizzle heavy cream over filling. Roll out remaining pastry to ⅛" thickness. Cut into ½" wide strips and top tart with lattice pastry. Bake in a preheated oven at 425 degrees for 30 minutes or until lightly browned. Cool on a wire rack. Serve slightly warm or chilled. Garnish if desired.

Serves 8 to 10.

• *Note:* Margarine may be substituted, but vegetable shortening is not recommended.

DATE TARTS

Sweet dark date filling in rich tart pastries.

PASTRY:
1 cup unbleached white flour
3 tablespoons chilled butter (or shortening)
¼ teaspoon almond extract
3 tablespoons cold water, approximately

FILLING:
1 cup chopped dates, pits removed
1 cup water
2 teaspoons unflavored gelatin
2 tablespoons cold water

Mix together flour, butter (or shortening), and almond extract. Gradually add water, adding just enough to form a soft dough. Pinch off pieces of dough and press into medium-sized tart pans. (If you do not have tart pans, you may use small-sized muffin pans.) Prick with a fork. Refrigerate until firm. Bake pastry-lined pans, placed on cookie sheets, in a preheated oven at 425 degrees for 10 to 12 minutes or until lightly browned. Allow to cool 5 minutes in the pans. Turn out onto wire racks, gently remove tart pans, and cool pastry completely.

To prepare filling, combine dates and 1 cup water in a small saucepan. Bring to a boil, turn to low, and allow to simmer, covered, an additional 15 minutes. Meanwhile, sprinkle gelatin over 2 tablespoons cold water in a small bowl, and allow to set 5 minutes to soften. Add softened gelatin to hot date mixture, and allow to cook at least 3 minutes while stirring. Gelatin will dissolve. Cool and refrigerate. When mixture reaches the consistency of unbeaten egg whites, spoon into tart shells. Store refrigerated. Garnish as desired.

Yields 12 to 14 tarts.

CRANAPPLE TARTS

Fruit-flavored tart pastries filled with apple, walnuts, and cranberries.

PASTRY:
1 cup unbleached white flour
3 tablespoons chilled butter (or shortening)
3 tablespoons unsweetened apple-cranberry juice, approximately

1 tablespoon cornstarch
1 cup finely chopped apple (peel, core, and chop apple)
¼ cup finely chopped walnuts (optional)
¼ cup thinly sliced fresh cranberries

FILLING:
1 cup unsweetened apple-cranberry juice, chilled

TOPPING:
14 whole fresh cranberries, approximately

Mix together flour and butter (or shortening) until evenly blended. Gradually add 3 tablespoons fruit juice, adding just enough to form a soft dough. Pinch off pieces of pastry and press into medium-sized tart pans. (If you do not have tart pans, you may use small-sized muffin pans.) Prick well with a fork. Refrigerate until firm. Bake pastry-lined tart pans on cookie sheets in a preheated oven at 425 degrees for 10 to 12 minutes, or until nicely browned. Cool 10 minutes on wire racks, remove tins, and cool completely.

To prepare filling, mix together 1 cup juice and cornstarch in a small saucepan until smooth. Bring to a boil over medium heat, stirring constantly, and cook 1 minute. Remove from heat. Add apples, walnuts, and sliced cranberries. Mix and allow to cool to room temperature. Spoon about 1 tablespoon of filling into each tart shell, top with a whole cranberry, and refrigerate to set. May be garnished as desired. Refrigerate to set.

Yields 12 to 14 tarts.

Tortes

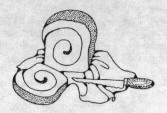

BANANA MERINGUE CREAM TORTE

Very light sponge cake filled with cream and sweet banana.

CAKE:
3 large eggs, separated (room temperature)
2 teaspoons vanilla extract
¼ cup unbleached white flour
¼ teaspoon cream of tartar

FILLING:
2 tablespoons unsweetened frozen orange juice concentrate, thawed
Creamy Topping (see page 104)
3 cups sliced banana (approximately 2 bananas)
2 tablespoons slivered almonds

Line 2 9"-round cake pans with wax paper and butter; set aside. In a small bowl beat together egg yolks and vanilla extract at high speed until lemon colored and creamy. Add flour, one tablespoon at a time, and gently fold into egg yolk mixture.

In another bowl, and with clean beaters, beat egg whites until frothy. Add cream of tartar. Continue beating until thick and firm. Fold together egg yolk mixture and egg whites just until blended. Pour the mixture evenly into buttered and wax-paper-lined pans, spreading batter to ½" from the pan edges. Bake in a preheated oven at 325 degrees for 15 minutes or until firm to the touch. Loosen cake edges with a sharp knife, gently flip out onto cake racks, peel off wax paper, turn right side up, and cool.

Shortly before serving, brush cake layers with orange juice concentrate. Prepare Creamy Topping as directed. Fold in sliced bananas. To assemble torte, place one cake layer on a serving dish, top with half of the creamy filling, and spread evenly over cake. Add remaining cake layer and cream filling. Garnish with slivered almonds; may also be garnished with additional sliced banana.

Serves 6 to 8.

THREE-LAYER FRUIT TORTE

Attractive fruit-flavored torte filled with creamy filling and colorful fruit.

CAKE:
1 cup butter, softened (see note below)
5 large eggs, separated (room temperature)
1 6-oz. can unsweetened frozen fruit juice concentrate (pineapple or apple), thawed
1 teaspoon vanilla extract
¾ cup water
1½ cups unbleached white flour
½ teaspoon baking soda
¼ teaspoon cream of tartar

FILLING:
Cream Cheese Filling (see page 108)
2 cups assorted colorful fruit (i.e., strawberries, raspberries, blueberries, kiwi slices, orange segments, peach slices, grape halves, cherry halves, etc.—all seedless)

TOPPING:
1 small-sized (11-oz.) can tangerine segments in unsweetened juice, drained

Line 3 9″-round cake pans with wax paper. Butter and set aside. To prepare cake, beat together butter and egg yolks until creamy. Add fruit juice concentrate, vanilla extract, and water. Beat well. Add flour and baking soda; beat just until mixed.

In a small bowl, and with clean beaters, beat egg white and cream of tartar until thick and firm. Fold together with fruit concentrate mixture just until blended. Divide batter evenly in 3 cake pans. Smooth batter evenly in pans. Bake in a preheated oven at 325 degrees for 25 minutes or until firm. Cool in the pans 10 minutes. Loosen edges of cakes from pans with a sharp knife, invert cakes over wire racks, and gently peel off wax paper. Cool.

To assemble torte, prepare Cream Cheese Filling as directed. Place one cake layer on serving platter. Top with ⅓ filling, spreading slightly past the edges so some will drip down the cake. Cover with a layer of fruit. Top with a second cake layer and repeat until ingredients are used, ending with cheese filling. Garnish cake with tangerine segments.

Serves 6 to 8.

• *Note:* Shortening is not recommended as a substitution in this recipe.

NEW ENGLAND APPLE TORTE

Light sponge cake layers smothered with spicy custard, and topped with apples and nuts.

CAKE:
4 large eggs, separated (room temperature)
1 teaspoon vanilla extract
5 tablespoons unsweetened frozen apple juice concentrate, thawed
¾ cup unbleached white flour
¼ teaspoon cinnamon
¼ teaspoon nutmeg
¼ teaspoon baking soda
¼ teaspoon baking powder
¼ teaspoon cream of tartar

CUSTARD:
Spicy Soft Custard (see page 104)

TOPPING:
1 fresh apple (peel, core, and thinly slice apple)
Walnut halves
Cinnamon

Line 2 9"-round cake pans with wax paper. Butter and set aside. To prepare cake beat together egg yolks, vanilla extract, and apple juice concentrate until light and fluffy, about 3 minutes. In a separate bowl combine flour, spices, baking soda, and baking powder. Fold into egg yolk mixture.

In a small bowl, and with clean beaters, beat together egg whites and cream of tartar until firm and peaks hold their shape. Do not underbeat mixture. Fold into egg yolk mixture. Pour batter evenly into cake pans. Spread to ½" from the edges and smooth. Bake in a preheated oven at 325 degrees for 10 minutes or until firm to the touch. Cool cakes in pans 5 minutes. Loosen cake edges with a sharp knife, flip cakes out onto wire racks, peel off wax paper, turn right side up, and cool. Prepare Spicy Soft Custard as directed.

To assemble torte, place one cake layer on serving dish, top with half the custard, another cake layer, and the remaining custard. Arrange sliced apple in a ring around the top, pressing apple into custard so that slices stand up on sides. Garnish with walnut halves and cinnamon.

Serves 6.

COCONUT MERINGUE TORTE

Three very light coconut-filled cake layers topped with vanilla pudding and fruit.

CAKE:
3 large egg yolks (save whites to use later)
2 teaspoons vanilla extract
½ cup water
¾ cup unbleached white flour
½ cup flaked coconut
1 cup egg whites, room temperature (about 7 large eggs)
¾ teaspoon cream of tartar

3 tablespoons flaked coconut

FILLING:
Vanilla Topping (see page 109)
2 cups sliced fresh strawberries (or your favorite fruit)

GARNISH:
1 cup whole fresh strawberries (or your favorite fruit)

Line 3 9"-round cake pans with wax paper; butter and set aside. To prepare cake beat together egg yolks, vanilla extract, and water for about 5 minutes until light and fluffy. Add flour and ½ cup flaked coconut a few tablespoons at a time, and gently fold into egg yolk mixture. Set aside.

In a separate large bowl, and with clean beaters, beat egg whites together with cream of tartar until stiff. Fold together with egg yolk mixture just until blended. Divide mixture evenly in baking pans, smoothing batter with a spatula to ½" from the edges. Sprinkle 1 tablespoon of flaked coconut evenly over each cake layer. Bake in a preheated oven at 300 degrees for 25 minutes or until browned and firm. Cool in pans 10 minutes. Gently loosen cakes from pans with a sharp knife. Flip over, gently peel off wax paper, and cool right side up on wire racks. Prepare Vanilla Topping as directed. Fold in sliced strawberries.

To assemble torte, layer cakes on a serving dish, topping each layer with strawberry-pudding mixture. Garnish with fresh whole berries.

Serves 6 to 8.

CHOCOLATE PINEAPPLE TORTE

Two light sponge cake layers filled with sweet pineapple gelatin and topped with chocolate icing.

FILLING:
2 tablespoons unflavored gelatin (2 packets)
½ cup cold water
1 20-oz. can unsweetened crushed pineapple
¼ teaspoon cinnamon

CAKE:
1 cup unbleached white flour

¼ teaspoon baking soda
¾ teaspoon baking powder
5 large eggs, separated (room temperature)
½ cup unsweetened frozen orange juice concentrate, thawed
2 teaspoons vanilla extract

TOPPING:
Chocolate Icing (see page 110)

Sprinkle gelatin over cold water in a small bowl and allow to set 5 minutes to soften. Place bowl containing softened gelatin over another filled with hot water (like a double boiler), and set aside while gelatin dissolves into a clear liquid. If hot water cools before gelatin has dissolved, discard and replace with more hot water. If you prefer, gelatin may be dissolved in a small saucepan over low heat. Whip crushed pineapple, fruit and juice, and cinnamon together in a blender until smooth and creamy. Add dissolved gelatin and blend until well mixed. Pour mixture into an 8″ round cake pan; refrigerate until firm.

To prepare cake, toss together flour, baking soda, and baking powder in a small bowl; set aside. Beat egg yolks 5 minutes at high speed; they will become thick and lemon colored. Beat in orange juice concentrate and vanilla extract. Fold in flour mixture. Set aside. In a separate bowl, and with clean beaters, beat egg whites until thick and peaks hold their shape. Gently but thoroughly fold in orange concentrate mixture. Pour batter evenly into 2 9″-round cake pans lined with buttered wax paper. Bake in a preheated oven at 325 degrees for 15 minutes or until just lightly browned around the edges. Remove cake layers from oven and cool in pans 10 minutes. Loosen edges with a sharp knife, invert pans, peel off wax paper, and place on wire racks to cool.

To assemble cake, place one cake layer on serving dish. Run a sharp knife around gelatin, place briefly in warm water, top with inverted cake layer and serving dish. Flip upside down so gelatin will slide from pan onto cake layer. Top with remaining cake layer. Refrigerate. Prepare Chocolate Icing as directed and spoon over cake. Store refrigerated.

Serves 6 to 8.

Warm Desserts

APPLE DUMPLINGS

Fill fresh apples with raisins and spice, encase in pastry, and bake in a tasty apple syrup. Mmmmm . . . mmmm good!

PASTRY:
2 cups unbleached white flour
⅔ cup chilled butter (see note below)
⅓ cup cold unsweetened apple juice, approximately

FILLING:
4 whole apples, peeled and cored

½ cup raisins
Cinnamon
Nutmeg
2 teaspoons butter

SAUCE:
1 cup unsweetened apple juice
¼ teaspoon cinnamon
¼ teaspoon nutmeg
2 tablespoons butter

To prepare pastry, mix together flour and butter. Gradually add apple juice, adding just enough to form a soft dough. Divide pastry into quarters. Roll each out on a floured surface to form a square (6" for small apples, pears, or peaches, or 8" for large apples). Hold one apple at a time in the palm of your hand and fill with 2 tablespoons of raisins, a pinch each of cinnamon and nutmeg, and ½ teaspoon butter. Place each apple in the center of a pastry square. Join the four corners of the pastry over each apple, and pinch pastry edges securely together to seal in apples. (Edges may be pressed together firmly with the tines of a fork for an attractive effect.) Place in a small baking casserole. Refrigerate at least 1 hour.

Shortly before baking, combine apple juice and spices in a small saucepan. Bring to a boil, then remove from heat. Stir in butter. Gently lift up dumplings and cover casserole bottom with sauce. Spoon remaining hot sauce over dumplings. Bake in a preheated oven at 375 degrees for 40 minutes. Baste dumplings every 10 minutes during baking with hot sauce from the bottom of the pan. To serve, place warm dumplings into individual serving saucers and spoon over warm sauce. May be topped with whipped cream, if desired.

Serves 4.

• *Note:* Shortening is not recommended in this recipe.

•Variations

Pear Dumplings: Prepare as directed above, substituting 6 pears for apples. Use pear juice in place of apple juice for sauce. Reduce cooking time to 30 minutes. Serves 6.

Peach Dumplings: Prepare as directed above, substituting 6 peaches for apples. Use pineapple juice in place of apple juice for sauce. Reduce cooking time to 30 minutes. Serves 6.

BANANA DUMPLINGS

Soft, sweet bananas are encased in pastry and topped with a warm, spicy pineapple glaze.

PASTRY:
1 cup unbleached white flour
3 tablespoons chilled butter (or shortening)
4 tablespoons cold water, approximately

FILLING:
2 medium-sized ripe bananas

2 tablespoons unsweetened frozen pineapple juice concentrate, thawed
Nutmeg

TOPPING:
Spicy Pineapple Glaze (see page 109)

To prepare pastry, mix together flour and butter (or shortening). Gradually add water, adding just enough to form a soft dough. Cut pastry into quarters. Roll each out on a lightly floured surface to ⅛" thickness.

Cut bananas in halves crosswise, brush with pineapple juice concentrate, and sprinkle with nutmeg. Place a banana half in each piece of rolled pastry. Loosely wrap banana with pastry, leaving room for banana to expand during baking. Pinch pastry edges together. Place dumplings on a lightly oiled baking sheet, seam sides down. Prick with a fork to allow steam to escape during baking. Bake in a preheated oven at 425 degrees for 40 minutes or until nicely browned.

Meanwhile, prepare Spicy Pineapple Glaze as directed. Keep warm over low heat. To serve place warm (not hot) dumplings in individual dessert saucers and spoon over warm glaze. Dumplings may also be garnished with a dollop of whipped cream or crushed pineapple bits. Serve immediately.

Serves 4.

BANANA PANCAKES DE LUXE

Very sweet orange-flavored pancakes are filled with bananas and topped with a creamy banana ice cream.

PANCAKES:
1 large egg
1 tablespoon melted butter (optional)
½ cup unsweetened frozen orange juice concentrate, thawed
¾ cup unbleached white flour
½ teaspoon baking soda
½ teaspoon baking powder

FILLING:
4 ripe bananas, peeled
Unsweetened orange juice
Ground nuts or flaked coconut

TOPPING:
Jiffy Banana Ice Cream (see page 43)

To prepare pancakes, beat together egg, butter, and orange juice concentrate until well mixed. Add remaining pancake ingredients. Beat just until smooth. Spoon ⅓ cup batter at a time into an oiled frying pan, spread out batter with the back of a spoon, and cook over medium heat until browned. Turn once. Repeat until 4 pancakes are cooked.

Meanwhile, brush each banana with orange juice and roll in ground nuts or flaked coconut. Place 1 banana in each pancake and roll up. Prepare Jiffy Banana Ice Cream as directed. Spoon over pancakes. Garnish with additional nuts, if desired. Serve immediately.

Serves 4.

ORANGE SOUFFLÉ

A hot soufflé filled with sweet fruit juice concentrate and cooked to a light custard consistency.

SOUFFLÉ:
1 tablespoon butter
1 tablespoon unbleached white flour
1 6-oz. can unsweetened frozen orange juice concentrate, thawed

¼ cup water
4 egg yolks
5 egg whites, room temperature

TOPPING:
Cinnamon

In a small saucepan, melt butter over low heat. Gradually stir in flour until a paste forms. Slowly add juice concentrate and water, stirring constantly. Cook 5 to 10 minutes or until mixture is slightly thickened. Remove from heat and cool to room temperature. Gradually add egg yolks, one at a time, and beat thoroughly after each addition. Beat egg whites in a separate bowl until thick and peaks hold their shape. Gently fold into orange mixture. Carefully spoon into a buttered 6-cup soufflé or casserole dish. Bake in a preheated oven at 325 degrees for 35 minutes or until lightly browned and firm. Serve immediately. Spoon into individual dessert saucers and sprinkle generously with cinnamon.

Serves 4 to 6.

• Variations

Pineapple Soufflé: Prepare as directed above, substituting unsweetened frozen pineapple juice concentrate for orange concentrate.

Apple Soufflé: Prepare as directed above, substituting unsweetened frozen apple juice concentrate for orange concentrate.

BANANA ROLL-UPS

Warm pastry pinwheels filled with sliced banana and spice, and baked in a sweet pineapple syrup.

SYRUP:
Pineapple Basting Syrup (see page 103)

¼ cup butter (or shortening)
½ to ⅔ cup cold water, approximately

PASTRY:
2 cups unbleached white flour
2 teaspoons baking powder

FILLING:
1 cup thinly sliced banana
Nutmeg

Make Pineapple Basting Syrup as directed; keep warm over low heat.

To prepare pastry, mix together flour, baking powder, and butter (or shortening). Gradually add water, adding just enough to form a soft dough. Knead gently until smooth. Roll out on a floured surface to form a rectangle, approximately 10″ by 12″. Cover pastry evenly with sliced banana. Sprinkle with nutmeg. Roll up, jelly-roll fashion, starting at the longer side. Pinch loose pastry edge to the roll, and square ends by pressing gently with the palms of your hands. Cut into 1″ thick slices.

Pour half of the Pineapple Basting Syrup into an 8″ by 12″ baking casserole. Place pastry wheels into casserole, evenly spaced and with cut sides up. Spoon remaining sauce over pastries. Bake in a pre-heated oven at 375 degrees. Baste pastries with sauce every 10 minutes. Bake for 30 minutes or until lightly browned. Allow casserole to cool slightly before serving. Serve warm in individual dessert saucers, topped with syrup.

Serves 6.

●Variations

Prepare as directed above, substituting your favorite sliced fresh or well-drained canned fruit for sliced banana. Also, ½ cup chopped nuts, raisins, or unsweetened granola may be sprinkled over fruit before rolling.

Toppings

BLUEBERRY SAUCE

A colorful purple sauce full of sweet fruit flavor. Great over frozen desserts.

SAUCE:
¼ teaspoon lemon juice
1 cup blueberries, fresh or frozen, thawed

½ cup unsweetened frozen pineapple juice concentrate, thawed
1 teaspoon cornstarch

Combine all the ingredients in a blender and whip until smooth. Pour into a small saucepan. Cook over moderate heat, stirring constantly as mixture reaches a boil. Boil 1 minute. Remove from the heat, cool, and store refrigerated.

Yields 1 cup.

•Variation

Increase cornstarch to 2 teaspoons if a thicker sauce is desired.

STRAWBERRY TOPPING

A colorful and flavorful topping made from frozen strawberries. Serve over cheesecake, custard, pudding, ice cream, or cake, and enjoy strawberries all year long.

TOPPING:
1 12-oz. package frozen whole strawberries, loose pack and sugar-free, thawed

2 tablespoons unsweetened frozen pineapple juice concentrate, thawed
2 tablespoons cornstarch

Drain juice from thawed strawberries and mix with pineapple concentrate and cornstarch in a small saucepan. Stirring constantly, bring to a boil over medium heat. Boil 1 minute; mixture will darken and thicken. Cool to room temperature and gently fold in strawberries. Cool and refrigerate until mixture begins to gel. Spread topping over dessert while partially gelled, and refrigerate until serving.

Yields 1 cup.

PINEAPPLE BASTING SYRUP

A sweet sauce used for basting baked fruit or hot pastry desserts. Also may be spooned warm or cold over desserts as a flavorful glaze.

SYRUP:
1½ cups unsweetened pineapple juice

¼ teaspoon cinnamon
1 tablespoon butter

Combine pineapple juice and cinnamon in a small saucepan. Bring to a boil. Add butter and remove from heat. Use as directed warm, or chill and spoon over dessert as a topping.

Yields 1½ cups.

SPICY SOFT CUSTARD

A creamy stove-top custard excellent over sliced fruit, as a torte filling, or layered with fruit in parfait glasses.

CUSTARD: 2 tablespoons butter
2 cups milk   2 teaspoons vanilla extract
4 egg yolks   ¼ teaspoon cinnamon
3 tablespoons cornstarch

   Whip together milk, egg yolks, and cornstarch in a blender or with a mixer until smooth. Cook mixture in the top of a double boiler over simmering water, and stir constantly until mixture thickens, about 5 to 10 minutes. Remove from heat. Stir in butter, vanilla extract, and cinnamon. Cool slightly.
   Spoon custard into a refrigerator container, and top with plastic wrap pressed firmly against the top of the custard. This will prevent the formation of a top skin. Refrigerate until thoroughly chilled. Serve as directed.

Yields 2 cups.

CREAMY TOPPING

A light, fluffy topping to use over puddings, casseroles, and compotes. May be flavored with natural extracts and colored with natural food colorings for variety. This basic recipe is more stable than the following substitutions, and is recommended.

TOPPING: 1 teaspoon vanilla extract
1 cup heavy cream

   Refrigerate bowl and beaters to chill. With electric mixer, whip heavy cream in a small bowl until slightly thickened. Fold in vanilla extract and continue beating just until peaks form and hold their shape. Use as directed, or store refrigerated a short while.

Yields 2 cups.

•Substitutions

Using Light Cream (Not Half-and-Half): Prepare as directed, substituting light cream for heavy cream. Be sure cream, bowl, and beaters are well chilled. You may beat in an unbeaten egg white for additional thickness.

Using Evaporated Milk (Whole or Skim): Prepare as directed, substituting ⅔ cup well-chilled undiluted evaporated milk for heavy cream. While beating, add vanilla extract and 1 teaspoon lemon juice. Beat until peaks form and hold their shape. (If it does not reach desired thick consistency, the milk wasn't cold enough. Simply chill mixture in the freezer a short while and beat again.) Additional extract may be added to taste. Measure out 2 cups and use as directed.

Using Powdered Milk (Whole or Skim): Combine ½ cup powdered milk, ½ cup ice water, 1 teaspoon vanilla extract, and 2 tablespoons lemon juice in a chilled bowl. With chilled beaters, beat at high speed until peaks form and hold their shape, at least 5 minutes. Additional extract may be added to taste. Measure out 2 cups and use as directed.

CREAMY FROSTING

This frosting is used primarily in cake decorating. It may be flavored with natural extracts and colored with natural food colorings. (See Cake Decorating, page 121, for additional information.) This basic recipe is more stable than the following substitutions, and is recommended.

FROSTING: 1 cup heavy cream
1 teaspoon unflavored gelatin   1 teaspoon vanilla extract
1 tablespoon cold water

Sprinkle gelatin over cold water in a small bowl; allow to set 5 minutes to soften. Place bowl containing softened gelatin over another filled with hot water (like a double boiler); set aside until gelatin dissolves into a clear liquid. If hot water cools before gelatin has dissolved, discard and replace with more hot water. If you prefer, gelatin may be dissolved in a small saucepan over low heat.

Beat together heavy cream and vanilla extract until peaks form. While beating, pour in dissolved gelatin; beat until thick. Use immediately or store refrigerated.

Yields 1¾ cups.

•Substitutions

Using Evaporated Milk (Whole or Skim): Soften 1 teaspoon unflavored gelatin in 1 tablespoon cold water for 5 minutes. Meanwhile, heat ⅔ cup undiluted evaporated milk in a small saucepan over medium heat until hot. Stir in softened gelatin. Cool and refrigerate until firm. Beat in a chilled bowl with chilled beaters at high speed until stiff and tripled in volume. Add vanilla extract to taste (1 to 2 teaspoons). Measure out 2 cups and use as directed.

Using Powdered Milk (Whole or Skim): Soften 1 teaspoon unflavored gelatin in 1 tablespoon cold water for 5 minutes. Place bowl containing softened gelatin over another bowl filled with hot water (like a double boiler); set aside while gelatin dissolves into a clear liquid. If hot water cools before gelatin has dissolved, discard and replace with more hot water. If you prefer, gelatin may be dissolved in a small saucepan over low heat. Prepare Creamy Topping, using powdered milk as directed (see page 105). After beating 5 minutes, add dissolved gelatin and continue beating 5 more minutes. Additional extracts may be added to taste. Measure out 2 cups and use as directed.

•Variation

Cream Rosettes: Prepare Creamy Frosting as directed. Press through a cake decorating tube or pastry bag with a star-shaped tip.

Use to cover pies, cakes, or pastries. Rosettes may be pressed onto cookie sheets, frozen, loose-packed into freezer containers, and stored frozen. Place on desserts as you wish, allowing rosettes to thaw slightly before serving dessert.

VANILLA FLUFF

A light and fluffy vanilla-flavored topping. Good in cream puffs and eclairs, or served as a light pudding.

FLUFF:
1½ cups milk
4 tablespoons cornstarch
1 teaspoon butter (optional)
¼ cup mashed banana (mash ripe banana with a fork)

¼ teaspoon lemon juice
1 tablespoon vanilla extract
½ recipe Creamy Topping (see page 104)

In a medium-sized saucepan mix together milk and cornstarch until smooth. Cook mixture, stirring constantly, over medium heat until it reaches a boil. Boil 1 minute. Mixture will thicken. Remove from heat, and stir in butter.

In a small bowl beat together mashed banana, lemon juice, and vanilla extract until smooth. Add to milk mixture. Stir well. Cover with plastic wrap, press firmly into the mixture, and refrigerate. (This will prevent the formation of a top skin.)

Shortly before serving prepare Creamy Topping as directed, whipping until peaks hold their shape. Beat chilled vanilla mixture until smooth. Fold in Cream Topping. Use immediately or store refrigerated.

Yields 2 cups.

•Variations

For a lighter consistency use 1 recipe Creamy Topping.

Lemon Fluff: Prepare as directed for Vanilla Fluff, increasing lemon juice to 1 teaspoon and adding ¼ teaspoon lemon extract.

CREAM CHEESE FILLING

A fluffy cream cheese filling that is delicious between cake layers, as a cake topping, spooned over fruit, and anywhere you might use whipped cream.

FILLING: ¼ cup milk
1 3-oz. package cream cheese,   1 recipe Creamy Topping (see
   softened and cut in chunks   page 104)

    Beat together cream cheese and milk until smooth. Prepare Creamy Topping as directed, and mix together with cream cheese mixture until firm and peaks hold their shape. Store refrigerated.

Yields 1¾ cups.

• *Note:* Imitation Cream Cheese may be substituted.

•Variations

Cream Cheese Rosettes: Spoon filling into a pastry tube and press through a star-shaped tip to form rosettes. An attractive topping to pies, tarts, and cheesecakes.

Lattice Cream Topping: Spoon filling into a pastry tube and press through a shell-shaped tip to form a lattice topping (parallel strips of filling overlapped at right angles by more parallel strips). Use to decorate pies, quiches, cakes, and tarts.

VANILLA TOPPING

A flavorful, creamy topping that may be spooned over fruit, dessert casseroles, and tortes. For variety, stir in well-drained fruit and spoon over desserts.

TOPPING:
1 tablespoon cornstarch
½ cup evaporated milk
½ cup water
1 teaspoon vanilla extract

1 recipe Creamy Topping (see page 104)
2 cups sliced fruit, well-drained (optional)

In a small saucepan mix together cornstarch and a little evaporated milk until creamy. Gradually stir in the remaining evaporated milk and water. Cook over medium heat, stirring constantly, as mixture reaches a boil. Boil 1 minute, cool, and refrigerate.

Shortly before serving, beat in vanilla extract. Prepare Creamy Topping as directed. Fold into cornstarch mixture. Fold in sliced fruit, if desired. Use as directed.

Yields 2½ cups or more.

SPICY PINEAPPLE GLAZE

A sweet pineapple glaze that is delicious over cake, warm fruit desserts, and ice cream. Serve warm or chilled.

GLAZE:
½ cup unsweetened frozen pineapple juice concentrate, thawed

1 teaspoon cornstarch
¼ teaspoon cinnamon

Combine ingredients in a small saucepan, and mix until cornstarch is dissolved. Bring to a boil, stirring constantly over medium heat, and boil 1 minute. Remove from heat. Spoon over dessert or chill and serve cold.

Yields ⅓ cup.

●Variations

Spicy Orange Glaze: Prepare as directed above, using unsweetened frozen orange juice concentrate.

Spicy Apple Glaze: Prepare as directed above, using unsweetened frozen apple juice concentrate.

CHOCOLATE ICING

A delicious chocolate icing sweetened with banana. Spoon warm over desserts. May be thinned with additional hot water for a thinner icing.

ICING:
3 tablespoons butter
¼ cup water
⅓ cup mashed banana (mash ripe banana with a fork)

¼ teaspoon lemon juice
1 teaspoon vanilla extract
2 tablespoons unsweetened cocoa
1¼ cups instant powdered milk

In a small saucepan combine butter and water. Bring to a boil over low heat. Meanwhile, beat together mashed banana, lemon juice, and vanilla extract until creamy. Add cocoa and powdered milk; beat thoroughly. Gradually add boiling water mixture and beat thoroughly after each addition so mixture is smooth and without lumps. Additional hot water may be added for a thinner icing. Immediately spoon over dessert.

Yields 1¼ cups.

●Variations

Chocolate Glaze: Prepare as directed above, increasing water to approximately ⅓ cup, or more, until glaze reaches desired consistency.

Chocolate Frosting: Prepare as directed for Chocolate Icing, using slightly less water. Spread immediately over dessert.

Carob Icing: Prepare as directed for Chocolate Icing, substituting carob powder for cocoa.

Carob Glaze: Prepare as directed for Chocolate Glaze, substituting carob powder for cocoa.

Carob Frosting: Prepare as directed for Chocolate Frosting, substituting carob powder for cocoa.

PINEAPPLE-COCOA ICING

Tangy pineapple and rich cocoa flavors combine in this sweet brown icing. Drizzle icing over cakes, turnovers, cream puffs, and pastries.

ICING:
3 tablespoons butter
¼ cup unsweetened frozen pineapple juice concentrate, thawed
2 tablespoons unsweetened cocoa
¼ cup instant powdered milk
1 teaspoon vanilla extract

In a small saucepan combine butter and pineapple juice concentrate. Bring to a boil over medium heat. Remove from heat and immediately stir in cocoa and powdered milk until smooth. Stir in vanilla extract. Allow to cool 10 minutes before spooning over dessert. Allow icing to set on dessert at room temperature, and store refrigerated.

Yields ½ cup.

•Variation

Pineapple-Carob Icing: Prepare as directed above, substituting carob powder for cocoa.

STRAWBERRY JAM

A thick, sweet jam full of flavorful strawberries. Spoon over cheese-cakes, into tart shells, and over tortes.

JAM:
1 12-oz. package frozen strawber-ries, loose pack and sugarfree, thawed

¼ cup unsweetened frozen pineapple juice concentrate, thawed

1 cup mashed banana (mash ripe banana with a fork)

3 tablespoons cornstarch

3 tablespoons cold water

Bring strawberries, including juice, and pineapple juice concen-trate to a boil in a small saucepan over medium heat. Turn to low.

Whip mashed banana until creamy in a small bowl. Add to straw-berry mixture and mix together until blended. Combine cornstarch and cold water together in a small bowl until creamy. Add to straw-berry mixture. While stirring constantly, bring to a boil over me-dium heat. Boil 1 minute. Mixture will darken and thicken. Cool to room temperature. Spoon over dessert and allow to set in the refrig-erator, or spoon in containers, allow to set, and later spread over desserts as a thick jam.

Yields 1 cup.

PINEAPPLE TOPPING

A sweet topping full of crushed pineapple bits and with a delightful light orange flavor. Great over cheesecake, pies, and cakes.

TOPPING:
1 tablespoon unflavored gelatin (1 packet)

¼ cup cold water

1 20-oz. can crushed pineapple in unsweetened juice

¼ teaspoon orange extract

Sprinkle gelatin over cold water in a small bowl, and allow to set 5 minutes to soften. Place bowl containing softened gelatin over another filled with hot water (like a double boiler). Set aside while gelatin dissolves into a clear liquid. If hot water cools before gelatin has dissolved, discard and replace with more hot water. If you prefer, gelatin may be dissolved in a small saucepan over low heat.

In a medium-sized bowl mix together crushed pineapple, including juice, and orange extract. Pour in dissolved gelatin and mix well. Refrigerate, stirring occasionally, as mixture thickens slightly. Spoon slightly thickened mixture into tart shells, over cheesecakes and puddings, or into dessert goblets, parfait glasses, and pastries. Refrigerate to set.

Yields 2¼ cups.

APPENDIX I

FANCY TOUCHES

With a little extra effort you can transform the simplest desserts into fancy ones that will surprise your family and friends. Spoon syrup over fruit-sweetened ice cream, pipe lattice topping over a pie, layer fruit in a gelatin mold, line a charlotte with lady fingers, or tint a cake with natural food coloring. Garnish desserts with colorful berries, slivered almonds, or whipped cream rosettes, and serve in your best goblets or fanciest china. Your creative touches will add a sparkle to desserts. Not only will they be tasty and nutritious, but also a delight to look at as well.

Helpful Hints

Use a Variety of Pans. There are many decorative and unusual pans available. Gelatin desserts take on a new importance in fancy, upright molds. Or chill them in individual tart pans, china tea cups, or Bundt cake pans. Pie crust pastry may be pressed into gelatin molds and baked in a hot oven (425 degrees) until browned. Simply spoon in gelatin-cream filling or unbaked pie filling for an unusual and attractive pastry-lined dessert. Spoonfuls of cake batter may be baked in individual tart pans, gingerbread molds, or custard cups (adjusting baking time appropriately). Bake pies in large tart pans for attractive, ridged edges. Bake and mold desserts in casseroles. Collect pans with scalloped and fluted edges, rippled sides, animal, oblong, and hexagon shapes. Use your imagination!

Line Pans with Fruit or Nuts. Before pouring in cake batters, line the pan with a thin layer of well-drained fruit, nuts, coconut, or dried fruit. Sprinkle berries over pie crust before pouring in filling. Line custard cups with dried fruit, fill, and bake as directed. Sprinkle gelatin molds with nuts or coconut, or line with pineapple rings. Always use well-drained fruit, choosing colorful fruit with complementary flavors. When lining cake pans, layer fruit sparingly so it will not interfere with the cake texture and proper leavening.

Add Colorful Ingredients to Batters and Fillings. Bright red cranberry halves, deep blue blueberries, and light yellow banana slices add not only additional flavor, but also exciting color to desserts. Chopped orange apricots, dark brown dates, raisins, and chopped figs may be stirred into cake batters, pie fillings, gelatin desserts, and hot fruit compotes. Well-drained orange and tangerine segments make attractive additions to puddings and creams. Begin by adding fruits sparingly to cake batters so they will not affect moisture content; too much wet fruit can cause the cake to be wet and heavy.

Layering Ingredients in Desserts. Rather than mixing fruits in pie or tart fillings, layer fruit for an unusual effect. Few desserts can equal the appeal of gelatin desserts that have layers of fruit, cream, and nuts. Layer fruit in baked fruit casseroles, dessert quiches, and cold fruit desserts. Serve when appropriate in clear goblets, casseroles, or turn out onto serving dishes to show off layering effect. Layer gelatin desserts in tilted goblets to produce attractive angled layers.

Use Natural Food Colorings. Available in health food stores and the natural food section of your supermarket, natural food colorings may be used to tint cake or cookie batters, toppings, frostings, ice creams, gelatin desserts (use several colors for attractive layering), and pastry dough. Flaked coconut may be soaked in a mixture of food coloring and water, dried, and used as a colorful, edible garnish. Fruit slices may be tinted with food coloring to change or accent natural colors. Since natural food colorings are derived from natural sources, they are not as concentrated as synthetic colorings; therefore, you may find it necessary to use more than expected to achieve soft, pastel shades. Occasionally, a natural food coloring will have a distinctive flavor of its own, and you may wish to add a drop or two of vanilla extract along with the coloring. Natural food colorings are indispensible in cake decorating, and turn everyday desserts into holiday ones.

Add Extra Sauces and Toppings. A variety of glazes, sauces, icings, toppings, and frostings are included in this book. They may be easily prepared and spooned over pies, ice cream molds, fruit cups, cakes, pastries, and warm fruit desserts. Glazes and toppings may be tinted with natural food colorings to contrast or complement colors. They may be served warm or chilled, and flavored with spices, extracts, and juice concentrates. Slivered almonds, whole berries, unsweetened granola, flaked coconut, and ground nuts may be sprinkled over desserts.

Dress Up Desserts with Lady Fingers. Fruit-sweetened lady fingers can be prepared ahead of time and frozen. Simply thaw, crisp in the oven, and use as directed (see Lady Fingers, page 9, for details). Line a dessert goblet with lady fingers and spoon in pudding, or place in a gelatin mold and pour in gelatin to set. Use as a garnish around fruit cup, whipped cream dessert, or sherbet. Add to charlottes and hot fruit compotes, producing attractive desserts ideal for the fanciest occasions.

Line Serving Dishes with Doilies. Thin paper doilies are available in a wide variety of patterns, sizes, shapes (circles, oblongs, squares, rectangles), and colors. Although white is most commonly used, gold and silver accent special occasions, as well as patterns and pastel shades. Place cakes, cookies, pastries, and individual tarts on doily-lined serving dishes. Serve goblets of pudding, fruit, ice cream, and hot fruit compotes on doily-lined saucers. Keep several standard-sized doilies available and use to complement your desserts.

Serve Desserts in Style. Spoon pudding into champagne glasses, ice cream into goblets, and fruit cup topped with cream into fancy English tea cups. Serve cakes and tortes on glass or silver cake stands, or serve on fine china platters—or what looks like fine china!

Light Some Candles. Just as candles add an elegant touch to dinner, so too, candles spark up many desserts. Cover a cake with candles to celebrate any occasion from a promotion to the first day of spring. Crown tortes, tarts, pies, and quiches with candles celebrating report cards, family get-togethers, and other happy occasions. Kids especially find candles in puddings, dessert casseroles, and even ice cream a delightful surprise. Who doesn't like to make a wish and blow one out?

Add Decorative Garnishes. Sometimes adding a decorative garnish to desserts makes all the difference in appeal. Sprinkling frozen blueberries over plain custard certainly perks it up. Or, add a fresh sprig of bright green mint to a pudding or creamy parfait. Spoon warm fruit casserole into dessert goblets and top each with a cinnamon stick. Arrange tangerine segments in flower shapes and decorate a cream pie. Sprinkle grated orange, lemon, or lime rind over whipped cream toppings, or sprinkle with cocoa or carob powder. Best of all, smother your dessert with pastry tube creations and have a ball doing it! (See Cake Decorating, page 121.)

Especially for Kids

Like adults, children enjoy desserts that are not only delicious, but attractively presented as well. You may find the following suggestions especially appealing to children.

Serve Finger Foods. Kids enjoy desserts that are easy to handle and individual. Little pastry crescents, turnovers, or cookies are easy for little ones to enjoy. Rather than a slice of pie, serve each child his own little pie (tart) and watch his face light up in anticipation. Bake hot fruit desserts in little individual casseroles. Mold gelatin and frozen desserts in little molds or cups to serve individually.

Brighten Desserts with Colors. Natural food colorings can create pink cookies, green puddings, orange cakes, and purple ice cream desserts. Tint frostings and glazes as well as flaked coconut to perk up desserts (see Use Natural Food Colorings, page 116).

Make a Face. Using bits of dried fruit, chopped nuts, flaked coconut, glazes, icings, and whipped cream, you can change a pastry, cookie, or tart into a happy face. Top pudding, ice cream, or cupcakes with silly faces and watch kids just eat them up!

Add Some Cocoa or Carob. Kids love chocolate flavor, so what better way to gain their attention than to lace desserts with cocoa or carob. Mix a tablespoon or two into batters (deleting an equal measure of flour from the recipe), fold into puddings and creams, whip into frostings, stir into glazes, and sprinkle over casseroles. Top desserts generously with chocolate or carob icings and frostings.

Serve Frozen Desserts. Kids love frozen pops, ice cream, and sherbet any time of the year. Whole seedless grapes and melon slices can also be frozen for handy, nutritious snacks.

Personalize Desserts. With an inexpensive cake decorating kit you can top desserts with your child's name, initials, or an announcement of the special occasion. Bits of chopped nuts, dried fruit, or flaked coconut can also be used to write "Happy Birthday, Scott," "Hi, Eric," or "Congratulations." What child wouldn't be delighted to find his name written on his piece of birthday cake?

Special Occasions

Desserts may easily be adapted to special occasions with just a bit of imagination. Cakes may be baked in preformed pans or cut into festive shapes (clowns, Christmas trees, hearts, Easter bunnies, etc.). Topped with tinted frostings, icings, or coconut, cakes celebrate any occasion from Halloween to St. Patrick's Day.

Christmas. Tint cake batters, frostings, cream toppings, gelatin, or ice cream desserts with red or green food coloring to welcome this special holiday. Bake in preformed pans, or cut cakes into Christmas tree, Santa Claus, star, or ornament shapes. Join cake pieces together with frosting and frost completely. Tree cakes may be decorated with bits of colorful dried fruit and flaked coconut "snow." Tinted

flaked coconut (see Use Natural Food Colorings, page 116, to prepare) may be used to draw a Santa Claus face with a red hat and
cheeks, pink face, and fluffy white beard. A simple rectangular or
round cake may be frosted in a festive color and topped with "Merry
Christmas" or "Happy Holiday" written in a contrasting color. A
cake decorating kit is an indispensible tool for fancy writing.

New Year's Day. This is the time for glitter and pizzazz, so bring
out your sparkling goblets, bright colored doilies, and silver-plated
serving platters. Top desserts with rich creams, chocolate icings, and
sweet dried fruit. Ring in the New Year with cream-filled cake rolls,
frozen mousse, and sweet little tarts amid colorful balloons.

Valentine's Day. Say "Be my valentine" with a heart-shaped cake
topped with pink frosting and coconut. Or treat your valentine to
a luscious fruit-filled torte. Follow a cozy dinner for two with cream
puffs or goblets filled with pink colored cream. Your extra effort will
say you care.

St. Patrick's Day. Tint batters, fillings, frostings, and icings with
natural green food coloring, and you're all set for this happy holiday!
Cut cakes, pastries, or cookies into shamrock shapes, or draw little
shamrocks on desserts, using a cake decorating tube. If you've an
artistic flair, add little elves or leprechauns.

Easter. Cakes cut into bunny shapes, frosted, and covered with
coconut are an easy and attractive Easter dessert. Bake a cake in an
oblong pan and let the kids help decorate the "Easter Egg Cake"
with colorful frostings, fruit, and nuts. A jelly roll cake can be cut
with a cookie cutter into little "eggs," covered with icing, and
decorated with frosting pressed through a cake decorating tube.
With a little imagination, cream puffs may be decorated to look like
baby chicks, and cookies like little bunnies.

Fourth of July. Ring in Independence Day with red, white, and
blue. A rectangular cake becomes a flag when frosted and covered
with tinted coconut or icing. If you prefer, use rows of strawberries,

coconut, and blueberries. Layer a gelatin dessert with strawberries, blueberries, and cream. Bake a cake or mold a gelatin dessert in a star-shaped pan. Press little tart shells in small star molds and fill with cream and fruit.

Halloween. Witches, goblins, and black cats can be drawn on cakes, cupcakes, tarts, and cookies. Mix red and yellow natural food colorings to make orange, and frost cakes and cupcakes into pumpkins. Decorate a cake to be a scary face, and cookies to be witches and trolls. Kids will be glad to come up with ideas of their own.

Thanksgiving. Warm fruit dumplings, casseroles, and roll-ups are a welcome addition to the Thanksgiving meal. An array of fruit pies and tarts reflect the down-home feeling of this family holiday. Puddings and sauces, layered in goblets, are a welcome dessert. Using a pastry tube, decorate cakes, cupcakes, and cookies with turkeys, pilgrims, and Indians. Few kids can resist helping out.

Birthdays. Any basic cake can be transformed into a fancy birthday cake when decorated with flair. A cake decorating kit comes with a variety of tips for forming rosettes, flowers, leaves, cake writing, and more. Combined with tinted frostings and sparkling candles, cake decorating kits allow you to prepare cakes that look professionally decorated. And what better birthday surprise!

Cake Decorating

Few skills transform everyday desserts into special occasion ones as easily as cake decorating does. Topping a cake with bright red roses, yellow daisies, and pink tulips, and threading the flowers together with colorful green leaves and stems, turns a cake into a garden of color and shapes. Cover a cake with rings of rosettes, orange butterflies, or a basket-weave pattern. Top tarts and pies with a lattice frosting topping, and crown puddings and creams with colorful frosting flowers. Eclairs may be topped with strips of cream and cream puffs with fancy rosettes.

Frosting. Whipped cream makes an excellent substitute for sugary frostings. It's easy to work with, has a creamy texture, and its white color readily tints to a variety of attractive pastel shades. Dissolved gelatin is often beaten into the cream to provide the additional stiffness necessary to work well through a pastry tube. Also, a variety of natural colorings may be added to the cream. Those wishing to frost with a lower calorie, lower cholesterol, or milk-free frosting will find a variety of substitutions available. (See Creamy Frosting, page 105.)

Cake Decorating Kit. An inexpensive cake decorating kit can be purchased from gourmet or specialty stores. It consists of a cylindrical tube, plunger, and a variety of tips. The frosting is spooned into the tube and presses out through the tip to form various decorations. If you prefer, a pastry bag with tips may be used. Beginners will probably find the less expensive metal cake decorating kit easier to work with.

Preparing the Cake to Frost. Allow the cake to cool thoroughly and brush off any crumbs. Center cake upside down on serving dish so top will be smooth. If cake does not lay flat on platter, remove and trim bottom as necessary. If you wish, you may slide pieces of foil or wax paper slightly under cake so that after frosting these may be pulled away, and serving dish is left clean.

Tinting Frosting. Natural food colorings may be added while preparing frosting, or a few drops mixed in as you proceed and select your colors. It is easiest to begin by frosting the cake in white and dividing the remaining frosting into small bowls. Tint each a different color and use as you wish. Remember, some natural food colorings used in quantity do have a distinctive taste, so check and add natural extracts if needed to improve flavor. Also, you may tint frostings with natural fruit juices (i.e., grape, blueberry, cranberry, etc.), but colors will be pale and it may be necessary to add dissolved gelatin to retain proper stiffness.

Frosting Cake. Prepare frosting as directed (see Creamy Frosting, page 105). With a narrow spatula or blunt knife, frost sides with a thin even layer of frosting and follow with top of cake. Refrigerate and allow to set until firm. Remove any wax paper or foil if used.

Adding Decorations. You may wish to sketch out patterns lightly on frosting with a toothpick before applying decorations or cake writing. There is no limit to the variety of ways a cake may be decorated. For ease in decorating, place cake on a lazy susan or swivel plate stand so that it may be gently rotated as you apply decorations. The following suggestions may prove helpful. (You may wish to practice using tips before applying frosting to cake; frosting used for practice may be replaced in the tube and used again.)

- *Star Tip.* Coming in various sizes, star tips produce rosettes. These form an attractive border along the bottom edge of the cake where it meets the serving dish. Also, a ring of rosettes is attractive along the upper edge where sides and top meet. Several different sizes and colored rings may be added. The entire cake, top and sides, may be covered with rosettes. Large rosettes may be topped with smaller rosettes of a contrasting color to produce flowers. Rosettes may be placed in a zigzag pattern up and down the cake sides. Frosting may be pressed through the star tip in a continuous motion to produce fancy strips of frosting used for borders and writing (if using a small-sized tip).
- *Leaf Tip.* Green frosting pressed through this tip produces delicate, lifelike leaves. Press out in abundance around flowers, and along stems and vines. If pressed onto the cake in a continuous streak, it produces a wavy border.
- *Shell Tip.* This tip is often used to produce a border along the bottom cake edge. By pressing out a small amount at a time (about ½") and overlapping slightly, one can easily create fancy shell edging. If you prefer, a continuous streak may be applied as the cake is slowly and gently rotated.
- *Writing Tip.* Not only useful for writing messages on cake, the writing tip is also used to produce flower stems and vines. Tiny dots can be pressed out to produce flower centers. Rings can be drawn on cakes, as well as patterns and designs. Strips of color can be pressed out and placed over other

decorations to accent. Rosettes may be topped with contrasting colored centers.

- *Rose Tip.* It is recommended that roses be formed ahead of
time, frozen firm, and placed on the cake as desired. This
works best for several reasons. First, even when stiffened
with gelatin, cream-based (or any of the substitute) frostings
are not as firm as sugary frostings and tend to soften in warm
weather. By preparing ahead and freezing, they are kept
firm. Also, it is difficult for the beginner (and even the more
experienced baker) to create flowers directly on the cake. It
is usually recommended that flowers be formed off the cake,
allowed to harden, and placed on the cake. This is difficult,
if not impossible, when flowers are made from a sugarfree
frosting since they are easily crushed. By preparing sepa-
rately and freezing, they may be easily handled and placed
on the cake with no mishaps. Simply allow to thaw out on
the cake and they will retain form.

Small round bases that are designed to be used for making flowers
may be purchased from gourmet stores. Or, you may simply cover
the top of small bottles (such as vitamin or aspirin bottles) with foil
and use these as a base for flowers, one flower per bottle.

Begin by pressing out a small amount of frosting in the center of
the foil upon which to build your flower. Make small overlapping
petals, beginning at the center and working out to the edges. Tilt
tip slightly to allow petals to open outward. You may wish to make
several practice flowers. When flowers are formed, gently slide foil
off bottle caps without disturbing flowers. Place flowers on a dish and
freeze firm. When ready to apply to cake, peel off foil and place
flowers as desired.

Storage. All decorated desserts should be stored refrigerated. In very
warm weather you may wish to decorate for a short while at a time
and refrigerate in between to retain shapes and avoid melting.

APPENDIX II

INGREDIENTS AND HOW TO USE THEM

Baking Powder is a leavening agent used in baked recipes. There are several types of commercial baking powders. Double-acting baking powder is widely available and preferred since most of the gas is released during baking, resulting in a light product. The less popular phosphate and tartrate baking powders release most of their gases at room temperature, so a delay in baking the product will result in its failure to rise properly.

Recipes in this book are baked with double-acting baking powder, and I recommend its use. If you prefer, you may substitute 1½ teaspoons of phosphate baking powder or 2 teaspoons of tartrate baking powder for each teaspoon of double-acting baking powder required; bake quickly after adding.

If you run out of baking powder, substitute ¼ teaspoon of baking soda plus ½ teaspoon of cream of tartar for each teaspoon of baking powder required. Approximately 1¼ teaspoons of baking powder are needed for each cup of flour used in a recipe.

Baking Soda is used to leaven batters containing acidic ingredients such as fruit, vinegar, buttermilk, or sour cream. Most of the gas is produced at room temperature, so batters containing baking soda should be baked immediately after mixing. Often, baking soda is combined with baking powder to produce a more stable product. Approximately ½ teaspoon of baking soda is required for each cup of fruit juice, buttermilk, or sour cream used in a recipe, or ½ teaspoon of baking soda plus 2 tablespoons of fruit juice for each cup of flour used.

Butter adds flavor, softness, and texture to baked goods. It also contributes to the "keeping quality" of desserts, acting somewhat as a natural preservative.

- *Chilled Butter* should be used directly from the refrigerator. This is often required in pastries and pie crusts for flaky finished products.
- *Softened Butter* is butter that has been left out at room temperature to soften. It combines well with other ingredients in cake, cookie, and other dessert batters.
- *Melted Butter* is heated in a small saucepan over low heat until liquified or melted in a heatproof bowl in the oven. Use as directed as soon as liquified.
- *Butter Substitutes* such as margarine may be substituted for butter in equal amounts. Solid vegetable shortening often may replace butter in equal measure. Occasionally, shortening is not recommended in a recipe requiring a large amount of butter, as such a substitution would result in a crumbly product. Usually, recipes state when shortening is not recommended.

Buttermilk lends a distinctive flavor to desserts. It is usually made from skim milk that has been innoculated with culture and allowed to ferment, producing the characteristically tangy flavor. When buttermilk is used in a recipe, baking soda is used for leavening. To substitute buttermilk in a recipe calling for fresh milk substitute as follows:

½ cup buttermilk + ¼ tsp. baking soda = ½ cup milk + 1 tsp. baking powder.

Carob is derived from a plant called St. John's Bread. It is an excellent substitute for chocolate or cocoa. Carob contains less fat and calories than cocoa, while supplying calcium, phosphorus, potassium, and a variety of other vitamins and minerals. For those concerned about caffeine, carob is completely caffeine-free. Because carob is naturally sweeter than cocoa, this rich brown powder lends a sweet "chocolaty" flavor to desserts. It may be substituted for chocolate and cocoa in recipes. (See section on Chocolate.)

Chocolate is a popular ingredient in desserts and snacks. Unfortunately, it is so bitter that large amounts of sugar are traditionally included in chocolate desserts to sweeten things up.

The same delicious chocolate flavor and rich brown color can be found in fruit-sweetened desserts by combining modest amounts of unsweetened cocoa with the sweetest fruits, such as bananas. Powdered cocoa is easier to work with than chocolate, which has to be melted before mixing into batters. Most recipes can be given a chocolate flavor by adding a tablespoon or two of unsweetened cocoa while deleting an equal amount of the required flour. This way the proportions of ingredients remain the same. If a recipe calls for 1 square (1 ounce) of chocolate substitute 3 tablespoons of unsweetened cocoa plus 1 tablespoon butter or shortening. Carob may be substituted for cocoa in recipes. (See section on Carob.)

Coconut may be purchased whole and grated for fresh coconut flavor. Choose a coconut heavy for its size and free of wet spots. Puncture each of the three eyes (small spots at one end) with a large nail. Invert over a bowl to drain out juice. Bake drained coconut in a 350 degree oven for 25 minutes or until shell cracks. Remove from the oven and cool slightly before cracking off shell. With a small knife, peel brown skin off white coconut meat. Grate dried coconut meat on a grater or in a food processor. Store refrigerated in covered containers or freeze for future use.

One medium coconut yields 3 to 4 cups grated coconut and 1 cup coconut milk. One pound of coconut yields 5 cups shredded coconut. Coconut may also be purchased already grated, but often it has been treated with additives and coated with sugar. Read ingredients before purchasing. Natural, untreated, grated coconut is available in many health food stores; 3½ ounces yields 1 cup grated coconut.

Cornstarch is often used as a thickener in puddings and sauces since it thickens without affecting the flavor of desserts. Mix cornstarch with chilled liquid, add to dessert mixture, and bring to a boil while stirring constantly. Boil 1 minute; remove from heat. Sauce may be served warm or cooled as recipe directs. If mixture does not thicken sufficiently, mix 1 teaspoon to 1 tablespoon of cornstarch with twice as much chilled liquid, stir into mixture, bring to a boil, and cook as directed. For thickening, 2 tablespoons flour, 1 tablespoon quick-cooking tapioca, or 1 tablespoon arrowroot powder may be substituted for each tablespoon of cornstarch required in a recipe.

Cream of Tartar is a fine white powder derived from grapes. It is a leavening agent and an ingredient in baking powder. Also, cream of tartar is often used in beating egg whites. It is added when egg whites reach a foamy consistency, and produces firmer egg whites that are more stable during baking. Approximately ¼ to 1¼ teaspoons are used, the amount varying according to individual recipe requirements.

Eggs add nutrition, flavor, and texture to baked goods. When beaten until foamy, they trap air and therefore aid in leavening during baking.

- *To Separate Eggs:* Over a bowl, gently tap to crack egg shell; remove half, leaving yolk in lower shell. Gently slide egg yolk from one half shell to the other while allowing egg white to drip into the bowl. When yolk and white are completely separated, drop yolk in a separate bowl. If any yolk falls in with the egg whites, use a piece of egg shell to scoop yolk out and remove. Egg whites must be completely free of yolk if they are to beat properly.
- *To Beat Egg Whites:* Allow egg whites to warm to room temperature for most volume when beaten. They must be completely free of any yolk. Always use clean beaters and bowl. Beat egg whites at high speed until peaks form and hold their shape. Mixture will be quite firm and thick. A dash of salt or cream of tartar may be added during beating to increase firmness; this is recommended when beaten egg whites will be folded into cake batters. They may also be folded into gelatin desserts, puddings, and toppings for added lightness and volume.

Evaporated Milk is whole milk with approximately 60 percent of the water content removed by heating. No sugar has been added, and when combined with equal parts of water, it can replace whole milk in most recipes. It may also be beaten to produce a low-calorie topping, replacing whipped cream. (See Creamy Topping, page 104.)

Extracts are added to desserts to increase flavor and appeal. Vanilla extract is often used in fruit-sweetened desserts because it provides a light, flavorful accent that brings out the natural sweetness in fruit. Lemon and orange extract are also used to enhance natural fruit flavors. Purchase extracts that are naturally derived and avoid adding artificial flavors to your desserts.

Flour recommended is unbleached white flour. Bleached flour may be substituted if you prefer. In general, flour provides the framework for many baked desserts while absorbing and retaining moisture.

Gelatin (unflavored) is free of sugar, artificial colorings, and flavorings. It combines well with fruit juices, thickening desserts without distorting delicious fruit flavors. Colored and flavored gelatin is not used in these recipes as it is very high in sugar, a source of additives, and nutritionally far inferior to desserts made with unflavored gelatin and natural fruit juices. Unflavored gelatin may be purchased in an economical 1-pound package and stores almost indefinitely. One tablespoon gels 2 cups.

Granola (unsweetened) is often available through health food stores. You may also make your own. Combine equal amounts of oat flakes, chopped nuts, flaked coconut, chopped dried fruit, and sunflower seeds. You may delete any foods you wish and vary proportions to suit your taste. Season to taste with cinnamon or nutmeg. Use as directed for cheesecake crusts or as dessert toppings.

Heavy Cream is approximately 30 to 40 percent butterfat. It doubles in bulk when whipped to produce a fluffy, lightly sweet topping that is an excellent accompaniment to fruit.

- *To Whip Heavy Cream:* Chill the cream, beaters, and bowl. Shortly before serving, beat cream on medium speed with an electric mixer until mixture starts thickening; turn to low, and continue beating just until peaks form and hold their shape. Flavorings (extracts, fruit juices, etc.) may be folded into cream. Do not overbeat as cream will turn to butter.
- *Overbeaten Heavy Cream:* If you do overbeat and cream turns to butter, whip in 1 or 2 tablespoons of light cream just until blended.
- *Heavy Cream for Cake Decorating:* Heavy cream may be whipped until thick and just starting to turn to butter for use in cake decorating. (See Cake Decorating, page 121.)

Instant Nonfat Dried Milk is made from fresh milk with the fat and water removed. It is excellent in baking, and can be mixed with water as package directs to form reconstituted milk. Also, dry milk whips up into an excellent low-calorie whipped cream substitute. (See Creamy Topping, page 104.)

Light Cream or coffee cream is used in recipes for slightly more thickening and flavor than whole milk. Although relatively low in butterfat, it can be whipped into a low-calorie topping replacing whipped cream. (See Creamy Topping, page 104.)

Shortening referred to in these recipes is solid vegetable shortening. It often may be substituted for butter and supplies a no-cholesterol alternative.

Skim Milk is higher in calcium and protein than whole milk, and may be substituted for whole milk in most recipes. It may also be reconstituted from powdered skim milk as package directs.

Sour Cream is prepared by adding culture to sweet cream and allowing it to ferment until the desired tart flavor is reached. Its distinctive tangy flavor is an excellent complement to sweet fruit. It should be added to mixtures slowly so that its strong acidity will not cause the other ingredients to curdle. If you are counting calories, plain yogurt may substitute for sour cream in most recipes. (See section on Yogurt.)

Whole Milk is used in recipes throughout the book as a source of protein, vitamins, and minerals. If you prefer, you may substitute as follows:

> 1 cup fresh milk = 4 tbsp. powdered skim milk + 2 tbsp.
> butter + 1 cup water
> OR
> 4 tsp. powdered whole milk + 1 cup water
> OR
> ½ cup evaporated milk + ½ cup water

- *To Scald:* Heat milk in a double boiler until tiny bubbles appear around the edges. Remove from heat and use as directed.
- *To Sour:* Spoon 1 tablespoon of vinegar or lemon juice into a measuring cup. Fill with milk. Let stand a few minutes; use as directed.

Yogurt is prepared from fermented fresh milk. It is a versatile and nutritious low-calorie substitute for sour cream. (See section on Sour Cream.)

APPENDIX III

FRUIT FACTS

Dried Fruit

Dried fruit is simply fruit that has had a large portion of water evaporated from it, therefore concentrating the solid portion of the fruit. It is a means of preserving fruit. Even though over 50 percent of the water is removed, the remaining fruit contains practically all the original vitamins and minerals, but in a more concentrated form. Though rich in nutrients, dried fruit is also high in calories, often 5 times higher than in the original fresh fruit. When combined with water and cooked, it regains most of its original qualities, and is very similar to fresh fruit in nutritional values and calorie content.

Many fruits are available dried, and among them are apples, apricots, bananas, currants, dates, figs, nectarines, papayas, peaches, pears, pineapples, prunes, and raisins. Most are available singularly or in mixed fruit packages. Dried fruit should be stored in sealed packages in a cool dry place. In warm weather it is best to store refrigerated. Dried fruit will keep approximately 8 months.

Dried fruit should be soaked in warm water about 1 hour and cooked as directed (see Dried Fruit Cooking Guide, page 133). If the fruit package is labeled "tenderized" less cooking time is required; follow package directions. When cooking fruits to be used as purées, add additional water and cook for a longer period of time; fruit should be a mushy consistency. Use as directed.

If you prefer, dried fruit may be cooked in natural fruit juices, instead of water, to impart additional sweetness and flavor. Grated orange, lemon, or lime peel may be added during cooking, as well

DRIED FRUIT COOKING GUIDE

Dried Fruit	Cover with Water & Simmer for:	Increase in Volume When Cooked
Apples	40 minutes	5 times
Apricots	45 minutes	double
Figs	25 minutes	double
Nectarines	45 minutes	triple
Peaches	40 minutes	triple
Pears	35 minutes	triple
Prunes	45 to 60 minutes	double
Raisins	10 to 15 minutes	double

as a dash of lemon or lime juice. Any extracts should be stirred in after cooking and fruit has cooled to room temperature.

Dried fruits have a wide variety of uses. They may be stirred into batters, mixed into pie fillings, pressed into cookies, sprinkled over fruit casseroles, and arranged in tart shells and baked as directed. They may be tossed into fruit cups, folded into puddings, layered in gelatin desserts, and beaten into toppings. Dried fruits make flavorful and attractive garnishes on cakes, pies, tortes, puddings, quiches, and cheesecakes. They can also be cooked or stewed in liquid to produce tasty warm compotes, purées, and fillings.

Helpful Hints:
- Dried fruit may be easily cut with kitchen scissors or a small sharp knife. Occasionally dip cutting implement in cold water to prevent sticking.
- Cut fruit into small pieces when mixing into batters so fruit

DRIED FRUIT YIELDS

Dried Fruit	Amount	Yields
Apples	8-oz. package	4 cups cooked
Apricots	16-oz. package	3 cups uncooked 5 cups cooked
Currants	5-oz. package 1 quart	1 cup 3⅜ cups
Dates	13-oz. package 16-oz. package	2 cups with pits 2½ cups whole 2 cups pitted 1¾ cups cut up
Prunes	16-oz. package	2½ cups pitted 2 cups cooked
Raisins	1½-oz. package 10-oz. package 16-oz. package, seedless 16-oz. package, seeded	1½ tablespoons 2 cups 2¾ cups 3¼ cups

will not sink to the bottom of the pan while baking. Tossing the fruit in flour before stirring into batter also encourages fruit to remain evenly dispersed in batter.

Apples. Dried apples are commercially available in 8-ounce packages. They are a good source of potassium, while also supplying phosphorus and calcium. They must be stored tightly covered to avoid deterioration of fruit quality. The addition of nutmeg, cinnamon, and a dash of lemon juice brings out the flavor when stewing.

Apricots. Dried apricots are sold only in halves. They are an excellent source of vitamin A and iron. Since apricots are naturally rather tart, they should be sparingly mixed into desserts. They may be cooked in pineapple juice, instead of water, to produce a sweet, flavorful cooked fruit.

Blueberries. Although blueberries are not readily available dried, you may easily prepare your own and use in place of other dried fruits in recipes. Simply spread fresh berries in a single layer on a baking sheet. Place in the sun during the day and a warm room at night until dry. Store and use as for other dried fruits.

Currants. Dried currants are tiny, seedless grapes that have been dried. Although they are slightly tarter than raisins, they are flavorful and may substitute for raisins in most recipes. They are a source of potassium.

Dates. Dried dates are available unpitted or pitted, whole or chopped. They may be pitted by slicing them lengthwise with a small sharp knife and prying out the pit. Pitted dates are delicious filled with peanut butter, cream cheese, or nutmeats. Chopped dates are a sweet and flavorful addition to batters, pies, tarts, and cookies. They supply potassium, vitamin A, phosphorus, and calcium.

Figs. Dried figs are an excellent source of iron, as well as supplying potassium and calcium. Chopped figs may substitute for chopped dates in recipes.

Prunes. Prunes are dried plums. They are an excellent source of vitamin A, and a good source of potassium and iron. They may be "plumped" in any of the following manners:
1. Steam prunes in a colander over boiling water, covered, for 20 minutes.
2. Cover prunes with cold water, cover, and refrigerate 24 hours.
3. Cover prunes with boiling water, cover, and refrigerate until soft.

Raisins. Raisins are an adaptable dried fruit, mixing whole into desserts from cakes to puddings. They are a good source of iron. Raisins may be "plumped" in either of the following manners:

1. Steam in a colander over boiling water, covered, 10 minutes.
2. Spread raisins out in a baking sheet, cover, and bake at 350 degrees until puffed.

Frozen Fruit

Frozen fruit is a convenient, nutritious source of fruit, though more expensive than fresh or canned. It is available loose pack and sugarfree. Blackberries, raspberries, strawberries, cherries, blueberries, rhubarb, sliced peaches, apricot halves, and a variety of mixed fruit combinations are available in frozen bags. They range from 12-ounce to 20-ounce packages. Store frozen until using.

Frozen Fruit Snow. Slightly thawed frozen fruit may be whipped in a processor or blender to form a fine "snow." It may be used in recipes as directed or folded into whipped cream or pudding for a tasty cold dessert.

- *To Slice Frozen Fruit:* Allow fruit to thaw slightly and slice while still firm.
- *To Thaw Frozen Fruit:* Follow package directions for thawing; usually 2 hours at room temperature or 4 hours refrigerated is sufficient.
- *To Freeze Fruit:* Many fruits are suitable for freezing. Simply place whole berries or sliced fruit on a baking sheet and freeze until firm. Lift off and into freezer containers with a spatula, seal, and store frozen.

FRUIT: RECOMMENDED VARIETIES

Fruit	Recommended Varieties
Apples	*Eating:* Red Delicious, Golden Delicious, Grimes Golden *Eating & Cooking:* McIntosh, Jonathan, Yellow Transparent *Cooking:* Rome Beauty, McIntosh, York Imperial, Rhode Island Greening
Cherries	*Sweet—Eating & Cooking:* Bing, Lambert, Royal Ann *Sour—Cooking:* Montmorency, English Morello
Figs	*Fresh & Dried:* Kodata, Mission, Brown Turkey *Dried:* Magnolia, Celeste, Adriatic
Grapes	*Seeded:* Almeria, Concord, Emperor, Catawba *Seedless:* Thompson Seedless
Grapefruit	*Seeded:* Duncan, Burgundy *Seedless:* Thompson Pink, Marsh
Oranges	*Sweet—Eating:* Navel, Parson Brown *Sweet—Juice:* Indian River, Valencia, Hamlin *Loose—Skinned:* Tangerine, Mandarin Oranges, Tangelo, King
Pears	*Eating:* Bartlett, Comice *Eating & Cooking:* Seckel, Bosc, Clapp Favorite, Anjou

FRESH FRUIT YIELDS

Fruit	Amount	Yields
Apples	1 medium-sized fruit 1 pound	1 cup sliced ⅔ cup grated 3 medium-sized fruit 3 cups sliced 1½ cups sauce
Apricots	1 pound	4 cups fruit
Bananas	1 medium-sized fruit 1 pound	½ cup mashed 3 medium-sized fruit 2½ cups sliced 1⅓ cups mashed
Berries	1 pint	1¾ cups fruit
Cherries	1 quart with stems 1 quart, stemmed	1½ pounds 3 cups stemmed & pitted 2 cups juice 2 pounds 4 cups pitted 2 cups juice
Cranberries	1 pound	4 cups
Figs	1 pound	2¾ cups ⅔ cups chopped
Lemons	1 medium-sized fruit 1 pound	2 to 3 tablespoons juice 1 tablespoon grated rind 4 lemons ⅔ cup juice
Limes	1 medium-sized fruit	1 to 2 tablespoons juice ¾ teaspoon grated rind

FRESH FRUIT YIELDS *(continued)*

Fruit	Amount	Yields
Oranges	1 medium-sized fruit	⅓ to ½ cup juice 1 to 2 tablespoons grated peel
Peaches	1 medium-sized fruit 1 pound	½ cup peeled and sliced 2 cups sliced 1 cup pulp
Pears	1 medium-sized fruit 1 pound	½ cup peeled and sliced 2 cups sliced
Rhubarb	1 pound	2 cups cooked
Strawberries	1 quart	4 cups hulled and sliced

APPENDIX IV

GUIDELINES FOR ADJUSTING RECIPES TO SPECIAL DIETARY REQUIREMENTS

Counting Calories

Although substituting fruit for sugar does substantially lower calories, the serious calorie-counter can lower calories even further with some minor alterations. The recipes in this book are specifically designed to provide flavorful, appealing desserts that can replace sugary ones without a loss of that rich, sweet dessert quality we look forward to. Therefore, special effort has been made to supply flavorful and convenient alternatives for weight-watchers so that they, too, may enjoy natural fruit-sweetened desserts while keeping the calories down.

Dairy Products. Following is a list of commonly used dairy ingredients that can be easily substituted with similar ones for a significant decrease in calories. (Further detailed information is provided in the Counting Dairy Calories Chart, page 141.)

- *Whole Milk.* Prepare instant nonfat dry milk as directed on the box and substitute for whole milk in recipes. This will cut calories by about 47 percent. If skim milk is substituted, calories are cut by about 34 percent.
- *Sour Cream.* Plain yogurt is an excellent substitute for sour cream both in flavor and texture. Since sour cream has over 3 times the calories in a equal measure of plain yogurt, yogurt is the weight-watchers choice.

COUNTING DAIRY CALORIES

Dairy Product	Calories per Tablespoon	Calories per Cup
Milk:		
Whole Milk	9.4	150
Skim Milk	6.2	99
Buttermilk	5.6	90
*Instant Dry Milk (reconstituted)	5.0	80
Sour Cream/Yogurt:		
Sour Cream	30.3	485
*Plain Yogurt	9.5	152
Cream:		
Light Table Cream	32	512
*Half-and-Half	22	352
Butter/Shortening:		
Solid Vegetable Shortening	106	1696
Margarine	101	1616
Butter	100	1600
*Imitation Dietetic Margarine	50	800
Cream Cheese:		
Cream Cheese	50	800
*Imitation Cream Cheese	35	560
Whipped Topping:		
Heavy Cream, Whipped	27.5	440
Light Whipping Cream, Whipped	22.4	385.5
Prepared Whipped Topping, (frozen)	11.9	190
Whipped Evaporated Milk, Whole	7.2	115
*Whipped Evaporated Milk, Skim	4.2	67

*Low Calorie Choice

- *Cream.* If a recipe calls for light cream, substitute half-and-half and cut calories by more than 30 percent.
- *Whipped Topping.* Low-calorie whipped toppings can be easily prepared from evaporated milk, dry milk, or purchased as frozen whipped toppings. Very significant calorie reductions can be achieved, as much as 85 percent, when these are substituted for whipped heavy cream. (See Creamy Topping, page 104.)
- *Butter.* Butter, margarine, and vegetable shortening are fairly close in calorie count. Imitation dietetic margarine does provide about a 50 percent decrease in calories, but it is not a natural product, and so, like margarine, it is not recommended.

Fruit. Although fruit provides low-calorie sweetening, individual fruits do vary in calories, and substitutions can further decrease the total calorie content of a dessert. A handy Counting Fruit Calories Chart (see page 143) is provided to supply information on calories per individual fruit, cup, serving, and pound. This can serve as a guide for choosing the lower calorie fruits.

- *Dried Fruit.* Not surprisingly, the significant calories supplied by fruit come in the form of dried fruit. This concentrated form of fruit is very high in calories. Figs, dates, raisins, and currants, as well as dried fresh fruit (i.e., apples, pears, bananas, peaches, etc.) all contribute substantially more calories in their dried form. When counting calories, either decrease the amount of dried fruit stirred into batters, completely substitute dried fruit with well-drained fresh fruit, or omit altogether.
- *Frozen Fruit-Juice Concentrate.* Frozen fruit-juice concentrate is another source of calories. It is used in moderation in many recipes because it does supply concentrated fruit sweetness in a convenient form. In the few recipes requiring a large amount of juice concentrate, it may be diluted slightly with water, thereby using the required amount of liquid while decreasing calories. You may find through ex-

COUNTING FRUIT CALORIES

Fresh Fruit	Calories per Fruit	Calories per Cup (sliced, chopped)	Calories per Serving (100 grams)	Calories per Pound
Apples	66	59	54	242
Apricots	18	79	51	217
Bananas	85	128	85	262
Blackberries	—	82	58	250
Blueberries	—	90	62	259
Cantaloupe	80	48	30	68
Sweet cherries	5–8	102	70	286
Sour cherries	—	90	58	242
Cranberries	—	52	46	200
Figs	30	—	80	363
Grapefruit	90	82	41	91
Grapes	2	110	69	197
Honeydew	495	55	33	94
Lemons	20	—	27	82
Limes	15	—	28	107
Nectarines	88	424	64	267
Oranges	77	118	49	162
Peaches	38	102	38	150
Pears	101	117	61	252
Pineapple	—	80	52	123
Plums	30	112	66	272

COUNTING FRUIT CALORIES *(continued)*

Fresh Fruit	Calories per Fruit	Calories per Cup (sliced, chopped)	Calories per Serving (100 grams)	Calories per Pound
Black Raspberries	—	98	73	321
Red Raspberries	—	82	57	251
Rhubarb	18	20	16	54
Strawberries	—	53	37	161
Tangerines	39	89	46	154
Watermelon	—	42	26	54

The above information is compiled from various U.S. Government Publications. Calories per fruit and per cup are approximate.

perimentation that fruit juice will substitute for fruit juice concentrate in many of your favorite recipes.

General Guidelines. The previous substitution suggestions will significantly reduce calories. The serious weight watcher may also prefer to choose desserts composed primarily of fresh fruit, baked fruit, or refrigerated fruit compotes and gelatins. These supply the good nutrition in fruit within a low-calorie dessert.

It should be remembered that cutting calories doesn't necessarily mean cutting flavor and dessert appeal. By choosing low-calorie substitutes in fruit-sweetened desserts, one may enjoy the best of all worlds—delicious desserts, nutritious desserts, and low-calorie desserts, too!

Managing Sugar Sensitivity

Although the recipes in this book do not contain added sugar, and thus serve the needs of the general population interested in a lower sugar content diet, fruit does contain natural sugar. Following are a list of suggestions to further reduce natural sugar content. It is imperative that anyone under medical care because of sugar sensitivity problems consult his physician before using these recipes (even with sugar content decreased further through the following suggestions) since acute sugar sensitivity may be affected even by natural fruit sweetening. Check with your doctor to determine what is allowed in your particular case.

Dried Fruit. Dried fruit is the most concentrated form of sweetening used in this book. Avoid the few recipes that use dried fruit as a primary ingredient (i.e., Date Tarts, Fig Bars, Date Sandwich Cookies, Cream Cheese & Date Crescents). In most other uses, dried fruit is stirred into batters, puddings, or pie fillings, and may be deleted. You may use flaked coconut, unsweetened granola (no dried fruit included), or chopped nuts as a substitute. When used as a garnish, substitute sliced fresh fruit if allowed, or chopped nuts.

Frozen Fruit Juice Concentrate (unsweetened). This is another fairly high source of natural sweetening. Instead of using full strength fruit juice concentrate, you may try half concentrate and half water. Often, you may substitute unsweetened fruit juice for concentrate, thereby decreasing natural sugar content by about 75 percent (usually one part concentrate plus three parts water equals natural fruit juice strength). It is best to experiment on each individual recipe to discover what level of sweetening works best.

Fruit Juice (unsweetened). Fruit juice may be diluted with water and used in recipes as directed. Also, it may be replaced entirely with water in pastries and pie crusts with little effect on the recipes.

FRUITS RANKED ACCORDING TO SWEETNESS
(NATURAL SUGAR CONTENT)

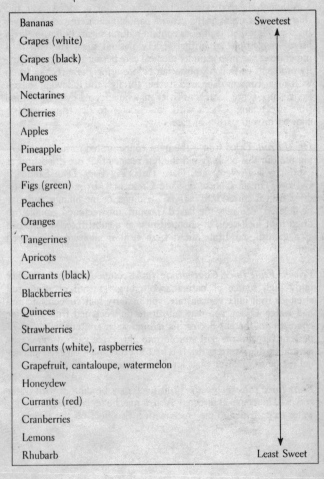

Bananas   Sweetest

Grapes (white)

Grapes (black)

Mangoes

Nectarines

Cherries

Apples

Pineapple

Pears

Figs (green)

Peaches

Oranges

Tangerines

Apricots

Currants (black)

Blackberries

Quinces

Strawberries

Currants (white), raspberries

Grapefruit, cantaloupe, watermelon

Honeydew

Currants (red)

Cranberries

Lemons

Rhubarb   Least Sweet

NATURAL SUGAR
CONTENT OF FRUIT

Fruit 100 grams	Sugars grams
Apples: eating	11.8
cooking	9.2
baked	9.6
stewed (no sugar)	7.9
Apricots: raw	6.7
stewed (no sugar)	5.6
dried	43.4
stewed (no sugar)	16.1
Avocado Pears: raw	1.8
Bananas: raw	16.2
Blackberries: raw	6.4
stewed (no sugar)	5.5
Cherries: eating, raw	11.9
cooking, raw	11.6
stewed (no sugar)	9.7
Cranberries: raw	3.5
Currants: black, raw	6.6
stewed (no sugar)	5.6
red, raw	4.4
stewed (no sugar)	3.8
white, raw	5.6
stewed (no sugar)	4.8
dried	63.1
Dates: dried	63.9
Figs: green, raw	9.5
dried	52.9
stewed (no sugar)	29.4
Grapes: black, raw	15.5
white, raw	16.1

NATURAL SUGAR
CONTENT OF FRUIT
(continued)

Fruit 100 grams	Sugars grams
Grapefruit: raw	5.3
juice (no sugar)	7.9
Lemons: whole	3.2
juice (no sugar)	1.6
Mangoes: raw	15.3
Melons: Cantaloupe, raw	5.3
Honeydew, raw	5.0
Watermelon, raw	5.3
Nectarines: raw	12.4
Oranges: raw	8.5
juice (no sugar)	9.4
Peaches: raw	9.1
dried	53.0
stewed (no sugar)	19.6
Pears: eating	10.6
cooking, raw	9.3
stewed (no sugar)	7.9
Pineapple: fresh	11.6
Plums: raw	9.6
cooking, raw	6.2
stewed (no sugar)	5.2
Pomegranate juice	11.6

NATURAL SUGAR
CONTENT OF FRUIT
(continued)

Fruit 100 grams	Sugars grams
Prunes: dried	40.0
stewed (no sugar)	20.4
Quinces: raw	6.3
Raisins: dried	64.4
Raspberries: raw	5.6
stewed (no sugar)	5.9
Rhubarb: raw	1.0
stewed (no sugar)	0.9
Strawberries: raw	6.2
Tangerines: raw	8.0

The above information is from McCance and Widdowson's *The Composition of Foods*, by A. A. Paul and D. A. T. Southgate, Elsevier/North-Holland Biomedical Press, New York City.

Other Ingredients. It is important to read labels and be sure that all ingredients are sugarfree—fruit juice concentrates, fruit juices, canned fruit, cocoa, carob powder, coconut, etc.

Flavor. It is also important to realize that as you decrease the sugar content of desserts, you will decrease the sweet taste that affects dessert appeal. You may wish to add additional extracts and spices (especially cinnamon and nutmeg), nuts, or coconut to enhance flavor and offset the decrease in sweetness. Remember, as you decrease fruit-sweetening, you are not only reducing the sweetness, but also the flavor of desserts. So add spices, dash of lemon, few drops of extract, or flavorful topping to perk up low-sugar-content desserts.

Substituting Fruits. Following are several charts which you may find useful in determining the sugar content of various fruits. You may wish to choose recipes using the less sweet fruits and to experiment yourself in substituting the less sweet fruits for the sweeter ones.

Adapting to Hyperactivity

Many nutritionists and physicians now believe that hyperactivity may be triggered off by diet in certain susceptible individuals. The most widely known diet for hyperactive children is the Feingold diet, published in 1974 by Dr. Benjamin Feingold under the title *Why Your Child Is Hyperactive.* This diet eliminates all products with artificial colorings, artificial flavorings, and the preservatives BHT, BHA, and TBHQ. Furthermore, products containing salicylates are initially removed and later reintroduced to note if any reactions occur. Some clinical ecologists cite food allergies as responsible for triggering off hyperactive behavior, especially allergies to sugar. Desserts may be modified to be free of artificial colorings, flavorings, preservatives, salicylates, sugar—all are sugarfree—and known food allergies. (If you are under medical care, consult your physician before making any dietary changes.)

Artificial Colorings, Flavorings, and Preservatives. These additives are widely used in our food system, but natural alternatives are available. Choose flour that is labeled "unbleached" rather than commonly available "bleached" white flour. Choose butter rather than margarine, selecting butter that is not dyed, but a light yellow color. Use 100 percent solid vegetable shortening. Choose extracts that are from natural sources without artificial coloring or flavoring. Purchase food colorings derived from natural sources at health food stores. Be sure to use pure fruit juices rather than fruit punches or fruit drinks. Read labels carefully on canned fruit and avoid fruit with artificial coloring and/or flavoring added. Read ingredients and choose only natural products.

DIETS FOR HYPERACTIVITY

Not Permitted	Permitted
Additives (Feingold Diet) Artificial colorings Artificial flavorings Preservatives BHA, BHT, and TBHQ	Foods without artificial colorings, flavorings, and restricted preservatives
Salicylates * (Feingold Diet) Apples, Peaches, Apricots, Plums, all Berries, Prunes, Cherries, Raisins, Currants, Tangerines, Grapes, Almonds, Nectarines, Coffee, Oranges, Tea	Breadfruit, Mangoes, Dates, Loquat, Figs, all Melons, Grapefruit, Papayas, Guavas, Pears, Kumquat, Persimmons, Lemon, Pineapple, Limes, Pomegranate, Bananas, Coconut
Allergic Foods (may cause hyperactive-type reactions) All foods causing allergic reactions	All foods not causing allergic reactions
Sweets/Sugar (may trigger hyperactive behavior) Cane sugar Also decrease sugar content from other sources (i.e., honey, molasses, fructose)	Natural sweetening in moderate to low amounts

*Initially not permitted and later reintroduced to test for possible adverse reactions.

Salicylates. Many fruits naturally contain salicylic acid. These fruits are initially eliminated on the Feingold diet and later reintroduced to test for possible adverse reactions. Fruit that are salicylates and are not salicylates are listed on the chart above. If a recipe calls for apple or orange juice (salicylates), try substituting pear juice with a dash of cinnamon or pineapple juice with a squirt of lemon. Turn an apple (salicylate) pie into a pear pie, and a peach (salicylate) quiche into a pineapple one.

Food Allergies. See Coping with Allergies, page 154, for further information.

Sugar. Thought by some to be the number one cause of hyperactive behavior, cane sugar is not used in any of these desserts. Be sure to choose canned fruit, juices, frozen juice concentrates, dried fruit, and coconut that is free from added sugar. It is added to many products you may not suspect. Read labels carefully.

Cutting Down Cholesterol

Those on cholesterol-restricted diets may adapt dessert recipes to be either low cholesterol or cholesterol-free. As the number of people restricting cholesterol intake increases, more and more products are especially designed to replace high cholesterol ones. In dessert recipes, dairy products and eggs are the primary source of cholesterol; therefore, substitutions are suggested. (If you are under medical care, consult your physician before making any dietary changes.) Many products now list cholesterol content, and ingredient listings are your best guide to low cholesterol products.

Butter. Although high in cholesterol, butter may easily be replaced with margarine. Margarine made from 100 percent vegetable fat contains no cholesterol, and replaces butter in recipes with no additional changes. Be sure to read ingredients, as some margarines are made from a mixture of animal and vegetable fats and do contain cholesterol. Solid vegetable shortening is often recommended as a suitable substitute for butter. Occasionally, especially in pastries, it is not recommended. (When inappropriate, it usually is listed as such.) Solid vegetable shortening contains no cholesterol.

Coconut. Since coconut is a fairly high source of cholesterol, it is advisable to replace flaked coconut with finely chopped nuts, bits of

CHOLESTEROL CONTENT OF FOODS

Food	Per 100 Gram Serving (milligrams)	Per 1 Pound Serving (milligrams)
Butter	250	1,135
Margarine		
all Vegetable Fat	0	0
Cheese		
Cream Cheese	120	545
Cheddar	100	455
Other (25% to 30% fat)	85	385
*Cottage, creamed	15	70
Egg		
Whole	550	2,200
*Egg Replacer**	0	0
*Egg Whites only	0	0
Milk		
Fluid, whole	11	50
*Fluid, skim	3	15

The above information is available through the U.S. Dept. of Agriculture.
*Lower cholesterol choice.
**Egg replacer is a powder available through health food stores to be used as a replacement for eggs in baking. Recipes may have to be modified when egg replacer is used.

dried fruit, or unsweetened granola. Often, flaked coconut is used as a garnish and may be deleted.

Cream Cheese. Cream cheese is used in cheesecakes, some pie fillings, gelatin molds, and a few toppings. Since it is fairly high in cholesterol, substitutions are advised. Cream cheese may be made at home by whipping low-fat cottage cheese in a food processor or with a mixer until creamy. A little low-fat skim milk may be added to achieve the creamy texture of cream cheese. This low-cholesterol "cream cheese" may be substituted for cream cheese in recipes.

Eggs. Probably the Number 1 food to avoid is the egg. Eggs are used in cake batters, quiches, custards, pastries, and more, to bring a cohesive quality to desserts, for thickening, and for flavor. Egg whites contain no cholesterol, so they may be used as directed in puddings, creams, soufflés, and gelatin desserts. Egg replacers that contain no cholesterol are available for use in baking; however, modifications may have to be made to recipes to accommodate the change. If the recipe only calls for one or two eggs, you may substitute egg whites from two eggs for each whole egg replaced.

Milk. Substituting skim milk for whole milk reduces cholesterol intake. Low-fat yogurt usually replaces sour cream with no complications. Evaporated skim milk replaces evaporated whole milk. Dried skim milk is lower in cholesterol than dried whole milk.

Coping with Allergies

Food allergies may be far more widespread than currently believed. More and more individuals are discovering that chronic fatigue, nasal stuffiness, headaches, aches and pains, and other common complaints may be triggered off by food allergies, often to their favorite foods. Adapting recipes to those with food allergies does require planning and some experimentation, but it is often far easier than anticipated.

Following is a list of foods used in this book that commonly cause allergies, with possible substitutions. (If you are under medical care, consult your physician before making any dietary changes.) Most of these substitute products are available in health food stores.

Milk Products. Allergy to milk is fairly common and, therefore, substitutes are available. Goat's milk in fresh liquid form or powdered form substitutes well for cow's milk. Also, soy-based powder that mixes into milk is available. Soy milk does have a distinctive

FOOD ALLERGY SUBSTITUTION CHART

Allergy to:	Substitution Suggestions
Chocolate Products	
Cocoa	powdered carob in equal measure
Chocolate	3 tablespoons powdered carob plus 1 teaspoon oil replaces each 1-ounce square of chocolate
Corn Products	
Cornstarch	arrowroot powder, rice starch, or potato starch in equal measure; half as much flour or quick-cooking tapioca
Baking Powder	corn-free baking powder (available in health food stores)
Eggs	
Whole	egg replacer; or ½ teaspoon baking powder, 2 tablespoons flour, plus ½ tablespoon fat may be substituted for 1 egg
Whites	egg replacer
Milk Products	
Whole Milk	goat's milk, soy milk, fruit juice, water
Butter	goat's milk butter, margarine, soy spread, solid vegetable shortening
Cheese	goat or sheep
Cream Cheese	goat or sheep
Whipped Cream	soy-based, nondairy

FOOD ALLERGY SUBSTITUTION CHART
(continued)

Allergy to:	Substitution Suggestions
Nuts	
Chopped Nuts	almonds, filberts, hazelnuts, cashews, pistachios, beechnuts, walnuts, pine nuts, hickory nuts, macadamia nuts, chopped roasted soybeans, flaked coconut
Wheat Products	
Thickening	quick-cooking tapioca in equal measure; half as much cornstarch, arrowroot powder, rice starch, potato starch
Wheat Flour	rice, potato, buckwheat, rye, oat, soy flour (may be substituted, but results are not predictable).

taste, so additional extracts or flavorings may be added to enhance appeal. Often, water or fruit juice may be substituted for milk in recipes without adversely affecting quality or taste. Butter may be replaced with goat's milk butter, soy butter, or margarine. Solid vegetable shortening substitutes adequately for butter in most recipes. Cream cheese made from goat's or sheep milk is available in health food stores, as well as a variety of other cheese made from these sources. Nondairy whipped toppings are available to replace whipped cream. Health food stores will often specially order products upon request.

Corn Products. Those with corn allergy can easily substitute other products for cornstarch. Substitute in equal measure arrowroot powder, rice starch, or potato starch. Half as much flour or quick cooking tapioca may also be substituted for cornstarch when used as a thickener. Corn-free baking powders are available through health food stores. (Most baking powders contain cornstarch.)

Chocolate Products. Those with an allergy to chocolate need not forego the delicious chocolaty flavor that is so appealing in desserts. Carob powder may be substituted in equal measure for cocoa. In batters and frostings, 3 tablespoons of carob plus 1 teaspoon of oil replaces a 1-ounce square of chocolate.

Eggs. Eggs are often used in cake and cookie batters. For those with an allergy to eggs, egg substitute powders are available in health food stores. These may be made from a base of potato starch and tapioca flour. Approximately 1 teaspoon egg replacer plus 2 tablespoons water equals 1 egg. You may need to adjust the recipe somewhat, depending on how many eggs are replaced and the interaction of the egg replacer with the other ingredients. Egg replacer may also be combined with water and beaten as a replacement for egg whites. (See package for directions.)

Nuts. If you are allergic to a type of nut or several kinds, you may find tasty substitutes among the following: almonds, filberts, hazelnuts, cashews, pistachios, beechnuts, walnuts, peanuts, pine nuts, hickory nuts, and macadamia nuts. Roasted soybeans are available in health food stores and, when chopped, are a tasty nut substitute. Coconut or chopped dried fruit may be stirred into batters to replace chopped nuts. Often, nuts may be deleted entirely from recipes without replacement.

Wheat Products. A wheat allergy is the most difficult one to substitute. Begin by choosing desserts that contain no wheat (i.e., puddings, gelatin molds, ice creams, sherbet, and hot fruit casseroles). Fortunately, there is a variety to choose from, with no substitutions necessary. In recipes where flour is used as a thickener, substitute an equal measure of quick-cooking tapioca, or half as much cornstarch, arrowroot powder, rice starch, or potato starch. Substituting another flour for wheat flour in cakes, cookies, pie crusts, and pastries has to be done on an individual trial-and-error basis. It will take adjustments, as no flour adequately substitutes for wheat flour in all recipes. You may wish to substitute rice, potato, rye, oat, buckwheat, or soy flour. It is necessary to substitute flours and combinations of flours, varying ingredients, until results are satisfactory.

APPENDIX V
MEASUREMENTS AND EQUIVALENTS

1 tblspn. = 3 tspn. = ½ fluid oz.
¼ cup = 4 tblspn. = 2 fluid oz.
⅓ cup = 5 tblspn. plus 1 tspn.
½ cup = 8 tblspn. = 4 fluid oz.
⅔ cup = 10 tblspn. plus 2 tspn.
¾ cup = 12 tblspn. = 6 fluid oz.
1 cup = 16 tblspn. = 8 fluid oz.
1 pint = 2 cups

Butter, Stick
  ¼ lb. = 1 stick = ½ cup =
    8 tblspn.

Butter, Whipped
  1 lb. = 3 cups = 6 sticks =
    2 8-ounce containers

Carob
  1 lb. = 2⅔ cups
  1 cup = 252 calories
  1 tblspn. = 16 calories

Cheese, Cheddar
  1 lb. = 4 cups grated
  4 oz. = 1 cup grated
  ¼ lb. = 1 cup shredded

Cheese, Cottage
  1 lb. = 2 cups = 16 ounces

Cheese, Cream
  3 oz. = 6 tblspn.

Chocolate, Unsweetened
  1 cup grated = 667 calories
  1 oz. = 143 calories
  1 square = 2 heaping tblspn.
    grated

Cocoa, Unsweetened
  1 cup = approximately 189
    calories
  1 tblspn. = 12 to 14 calories
  1 lb. = 4 cups

Coconut
  1 medium = 3 to 4 cups grated
  1 cup grated = 1⅓ cups flaked
  3½ oz. flaked = 1⅓ cups

Cream, Heavy
  1 pint = 4 cups, whipped

Eggs, Whole
  2 large = 3 small
  3 medium = ½ cup
  5 large = 1 cup

Egg, Whites
  1 cup = 8 to 10 whites

Egg, Yolks
  1 cup = 12 to 14 yolks

Flour, All-Purpose
  1 lb. = 4 cups
  4 oz. = 1 cup

Gelatin, Unflavored
  1 packet = 1 tblspn.

Leavening
  1 oz. baking soda = 2 tblspn.
  1 oz. cream of tartar = 3 tblspn.
  1 oz. baking powder = 2⅔ tblspn.

Milk, Evaporated
  14½ oz. can = 1⅔ cups = 3⅓ cups milk
  6 oz. can = ⅔ cup = 1⅓ cups milk

Milk, Dry
  1 lb. = 4 cups

Pumpkin
  1 16-oz. can = 2 cups

Shortening, Solid
  1 lb. = 2⅓ cups
  1 cup = ⅔ cup oil

Nuts, In Shell
Almonds
  1 lb. = 1 to 1⅓ cups, nutmeats = ⅔ cup, shelled
Peanuts
  1 lb. = 2 cups, nutmeats
Pecans
  1 lb. = 2¼ cups, nutmeats = 1¼ cups, shelled
Walnuts
  1 lb. = 2 cups, nutmeats = 1¾ cups, shelled

Nuts, Shelled
Almonds
  1 lb. = 3 cups nutmeats
Peanuts
  1 lb. = 3½ cups nutmeats
Pecans
  1 lb. = 4 cups nutmeats
Walnuts
  1 lb. = 4½ cups nutmeats

APPENDIX VI
RECOMMENDED READING

Allergy

Crook, William G. *Tracking Down Hidden Food Allergy.* Jackson, Tenn.: Professional Books, 1978.

Mandell, Marshall, and Scanlon, Lynne W. *Dr. Mandell's 5 Day Allergy Relief System.* New York: Thomas Y. Crowell Publishers, 1979.

Philpott, William H., and Kalita, Dwight K. *Brain Allergies: The Psychonutrient Connection.* New Canaan, Conn.: Keats Publishing, 1980.

Randolph, Theron G., and Moss, Ralph W. *An Alternative Approach to Allergies.* New York: Bantam Books, 1982.

Sheinkin, D., Schachter, M., and Hutton, R. *The Food Connection.* New York: The Bobbs-Merrill Co., 1979.

Calories

Consumers Guide Editors. *The Dieter's Complete Guide to Calories, Carbohydrates, Sodium, Fats and Cholesterol.* New York: Fawcett Books, 1981.

Fredericks, Carlton. *Carlton Fredericks' Caloric and Carbohydrate Guide.* New York: Pocket Books, 1977.

Kraus, Barbara. *Barbara Kraus 1979 Caloric Guide to Brand Names & Basic Foods.* New York: New American Library, 1979.

Children

Davis, Adelle. *Let's Have Healthy Children.* New York: Harcourt Brace and World, 1954.

Sloan, Sara. *Nutritional Parenting.* Passwater, Richard A. and Mindell, Earl R., eds. New Canaan, Conn.: Keats Publishing, 1982.

Smith, Lendon. *Feed Your Kids Right: Dr. Smith's Program For Your Child's Total Health.* New York: McGraw-Hill Book Co., 1979.

Smith, Lendon. *Foods For Healthy Kids.* New York: Berkley Publishing, 1982.

Cholesterol

ABC Milligram Cholesterol Diet Guide. Miami Beach, Fla.: Merit Publications, 1977.

Alphabetical Diet Guide Cholesterol Ratings. Miami Beach, Fla.: Merit Publications, 1976.

Cholesterol Diet Guide Carbohydrate. Miami Beach, Fla.: Merit Publications, 1974.

Jones, Jeanne. *Diet for a Happy Heart.* San Francisco, Calif.: One Hundred One Publications, 1975.

Hyperactivity

Crook, William G. *Can Your Child Read? Is He Hyperactive?* Jackson, Tenn.: Professional Books, 1977.

Feingold, Helene, and Feingold, Ben. *The Feingold Cookbook for Hyperactive Children.* New York: Random House, 1979

Feingold, Ben F. *Why Your Child Is Hyperactive.* New York: Random House, 1974.

Rapp, Doris J. *Allergies and the Hyperactive Child.* New York: Sovereign Books, 1979.

Smith, Lendon. *Improving Your Child's Behavior Chemistry.* New York: Pocket Books, 1980.

Nutrition

Bernarde, Melvin A. *The Chemicals We Eat.* New York: American Heritage Press, 1971.

Cheraskin, E., Ringsdorf, W.M., and Brecher, Arline. *Psycho-Dietetics.* New York: Bantam Books, 1974.

Fredericks, Carlton, and Bailey, Herbert. *Food Facts & Fallacies.* New York: Arco Publishing, 1968.

Hoffer, Abram, and Walker, Morton. *Orthomolecular Nutrition.* New Cannan, Conn.: Keats Publishing, 1978.

U.S. Department of Agriculture. *The Composition of Foods, Agricultural Handbook No. 8.* Washington D.C.: Government Printing Office, 1963.

Sugar Sensitivity

Abrahamson, E.M., and Pezet, A.W. *Body, Mind, and Sugar.* Moonachie, N.J.: Pyramid Publications/Harcourt Brace Jovanovich, 1971.

Airola, Paavo. *Hypoglycemia: A Better Approach.* Phoenix, Ariz.: Health Plus Publications, 1977.

Dufty, William. *Sugar Blues*. New York: Warner Books, 1975.

Fredericks, Carlton, and Goodman, Herman. *Low Blood Sugar and You*. New York: Constellation International, 1969.

Hunter, Beatrice T. *The Sugar Trap & How To Avoid It*. Boston, Mass.: Houghton Mifflin Co., 1982.

Krilanovich, Nicholas. *No Sugar Added or Redesigning Our Children's Future*. Santa Barbara, Calif.: November Books, 1982.

INDEX

Great Cooking
at Your Fingertips

THE CHICKEN GOURMET
by Ferdie Blackburn
A mouth-watering celebration of over 100 international and classic recipes for family and festive occasions.
_____ 90088-0 $3.50   _____90089-9 $4.50 Can.

THE BOOK OF WHOLE GRAINS
by Marlene Anne Bumgarner
Hundreds of great-tasting, health-giving recipes.
_____ 90072-4 $4.95 U.S.   _____ 90073-2 $6.25 Can.

THE FOOD ALLERGY COOKBOOK
by the Allergy Information Association
Breakthrough recipes that bring great taste back to restricted diets—each recipe free of two or more of the most common allergens.
_____ 90185-2 $4.95 U.S.

ST. MARTIN'S PRESS—MAIL SALES
175 Fifth Avenue, New York, NY 10010

Please send me the book(s) I have checked above. I am enclosing a check or money order (not cash) for $_____ plus 75¢ per order to cover postage and handling (New York residents add applicable sales tax).

Name _____

Address _____

City _____ State_____ Zip Code_____
Allow at least 4 to 6 weeks for delivery

HERE'S HELP...

MARY ELLEN'S HELP YOURSELF DIET PLAN
"The one-and-only good plan...presented by a funny, practical lady." —*Kirkus Reviews*
_____ 90237-9 $2.95 U.S.   _____ 90238-7 $3.50 Can.

WHEN YOUR CHILD DRIVES YOU CRAZY
by Eda LeShan
Full of warmth and wisdom, this guide offers sensible advice spiced with humor on how to weather the storms of parenting.
_____ 90387-1 $4.50 U.S.   _____ 90392-8 $5.75 Can.

HOW TO GET A MAN TO MAKE A COMMITMENT
by Bonnie Barnes and Tisha Clark
Take charge of your life—discover the two-week plan to get your relationship just where *you* want it to be!
_____ 90189-5 $3.95 U.S.   _____ 90190-9 $4.95 Can.